CAMBRIDGE UNIVERSITY PRESS

UNIVERSITY *of* CAMBRIDGE
ESOL Examinations

Cambridge English

Compact
Preliminary
for Schools

Teacher's Book

Sue Elliott and Amanda Thomas

CAMBRIDGE UNIVERSITY PRESS
Cambridge, New York, Melbourne, Madrid, Cape Town,
Singapore, São Paulo, Delhi, Mexico City

Cambridge University Press
The Edinburgh Building, Cambridge CB2 8RU, UK

www.cambridge.org
Information on this title: www.cambridge.org/9781107610279

First published 2013
Reprinted 2013

Printed in Italy by L.E.G.O. S.p.A.

A catalogue record for this publication is available from the British Library

ISBN 978-1-107-69409-5 Student's Book without answers with CD-ROM
ISBN 978-1-107-61027-9 Teacher's Book
ISBN 978-1-107-63539-5 Workbook without answers with Audio CD
ISBN 978-1-107-66714-3 Student's Pack
ISBN 978-1-107-63262-2 Class Audio CD
ISBN 978-1-107-69233-6 Classware DVD-ROM

Contents

Map of the units

UNIT	TOPICS	GRAMMAR	VOCABULARY
1 All about me!	Giving personal information Being at school	Present simple & present continuous *-ing* forms	School subjects Sports facilities School rooms School collocations
2 Winning & losing	Sport Hobbies & leisure	Past simple Past continuous	Phrasal verbs
3 Let's shop!	Clothes Shopping	Order of adjectives Comparing	
4 Relax!	Personal feelings Entertainment & media	Present perfect	
5 Extreme diets	Food & drink Health	Future forms	Food & drink Phrasal verbs with *go*
6 My home	House & home Places & buildings	*used to* Verbs followed by infinitive / *-ing* form *do, make, go, have*	Weather People Home Places
7 Wild at heart	The natural world Environment	Past perfect	Animals Natural world Weather
8 We're off!	Transport Travel & holidays	First & second conditional	

READING	WRITING	LISTENING	SPEAKING
Part 2: Finding an e-pal Part 5: School in 15th-century England	Part 2: Notes & emails Linking words Beginnings & endings Punctuation	Part 4: Talking about a new building for school	Part 1: Questions – asking and answering about school
Part 3: The history of BMX biking Part 5: The importance of team games	Part 3: Planning a story Correcting mistakes	Part 3: A talk about a special sports school	Part 2: A visit to a sports activity centre Agreeing and disagreeing
Part 5: An article about Harrods Part 1: Shopping	Part 3: Using pronouns who, which, where Pronouns for reference	Part 2: An interview with two young clothes designers	Part 4: Talking about places to shop
Part 4: My favourite movies Part 5: Learning to rock	Part 1: just / yet / already Word-building	Part 1: Short extracts about entertainment	Part 3: Describing people
Part 1: Food & health Part 5: Should we eat less meat?	Part 2: Modal verbs: suggesting, offering, requesting	Part 3: A talk about an extreme camping trip	Part 1: Questions – asking and answering about family and friends
Part 4: My home is a windmill Part 5: The pyramids in Egypt	Part 3: Linking words	Part 1: Seven short extracts	Part 2: Giving opinions, making suggestions, asking for opinions Things to take on a school trip to a castle
Part 5: The world's most dangerous animal Part 2: Charities working to help the environment	Part 1: Reported speech	Part 2: An interview with a zookeeper	Part 3: Describing animals and places
Part 3: My submarine trip Part 5: Holidays in space	Part 2: Describing a photo	Part 4: A conversation about a horse-riding holiday	Part 4: Talking about a holiday

1 All about me!

Unit objectives

PET TOPICS	personal identification, school
GRAMMAR	present simple and present continuous, *-ing* forms
VOCABULARY	words to describe selves, likes and dislikes and school
READING	Part 2: matching personal descriptors with short texts Part 5: gap-filling
WRITING	Part 2: notes and emails
LISTENING	Part 4: true / false questions
SPEAKING	Part 1: giving personal information

Giving personal information

Reading

Part 2

1   Introduce the idea of e-pals and ask students if they've got one or if they have ever thought of having one. Which country would they like an e-pal from? What kind of information could they write about themselves? (e.g. family, home, school, hobbies and interests). Make a list on the board. Students read about Mark to see if he wrote about any of the topics suggested on the board.

2   Ask them to read the text about Mark again and then, without looking, try to remember information about him. Get them to cover the text and see if they can answer the questions about him in pairs without looking at the text.

> **Answers**
>
> *Age?* 14
> *From?* Canada
> *School?* High school
> *Favourite lesson?* Art
> *What does he like doing in his free time?* drawing, using his computer, writing songs on his guitar
> *What sort of person is he?* friendly, tidy

3   Ask students to describe the two pictures to each other in pairs. Put any keys words on the board, e.g. *tidy / untidy*. They then decide which room is Mark's. Ask them to give reasons e.g. *I think Mark's room is B because it is tidy and there aren't many books on the shelves. Also there is a guitar and paper and pens for drawing. I don't think it's A because Mark is tidy and doesn't like football.*

> **Answer**
>
> Mark's room is B.

4   Students underline the details and then decide which of the three people is the most similar to Mark. Which one would be the best e-pal for him? (Cris)

> **Answers**
>
> Tom: sending emails, playing computer games
> Cris: someone who's lived in a different country, writing music, being a member of a band
> Sam: someone who is friendly and loves animals

Exam task

1   Read the Exam tip with the students and remind them that the classmates' requirements must match the e-pals' details completely. As in the previous practice exercise, they should be able to underline three pieces of matching information in each answer they choose. Remind them that they won't necessarily find the answer by 'wordspotting', i.e. matching the same words in the people descriptors and in the short texts.

> **Answers**
>
> 1 F
> 2 C
> 3 H
> 4 E
> 5 D

Further practice

When they have finished the exercise, ask students what they would write about themselves. Get them to discuss it in pairs, and then write a few lines about themselves and their hobbies and interests. Mark describes himself as friendly. Which positive adjectives would they use to describe themselves? Here are some examples – can students add any more?

creative	kind	confident
easy going	cheerful	sociable
generous	honest	reliable
patient	positive	polite

> See the Workbook and CD ROM for further vocabulary practice.

Being at school

Listening

Part 4

1   Read through the words with the students and check pronunciation. Let them work in pairs to classify the words.

When students have finished the exercise, see what they can add to the lists, e.g.

Subjects: physics, chemistry, sport

Sports facilities: gym, athletics field

Rooms: staff room, IT room, art room

Check that they can spell the words correctly, and that they note down new words in a vocabulary record book. A few spellings can be given at the beginning of each lesson, as part of a review.

Answers

Subjects: history, maths, biology, languages, geography, IT
Sports facilities: tennis courts, swimming pool, football pitch
Rooms: office, canteen, hall, reception, science lab, library

2 Students work in pairs to describe their school. Monitor and go over any mistakes at the end of the activity.

3 🔘 02 Read through the words in the chart with the students and check they understand what they have to do. Play the CD.

Answers

	☺	☹		☺	☹
canteen		✓	art room	✓	
gym	✓		science lab		✓
playground		✓	garden	✓	
swimming pool	✓		Sarah's classroom	✓	

Recording script

The first school that I attended until I was 11 was quite small. I remember we used to go in the front door, into a long corridor with rooms on either side. The first room on the left was the science lab. I didn't look forward to going there as I was no good at science then! The room next door was my classroom, a lovely bright room with yellow walls, and a door that went outside into the garden. I was always happy when we could go out there. At the end of a path was the canteen. Nobody really liked eating in there, including me – it was always quite dark. Opposite my classroom, on the other side of the corridor, was my favourite place, the art room. It was just next to the gym, where I used to love going to classes. The door from the art room went into a playground. I often fell over there when I was playing, so I was never very fond of it! And even though we were a small school, we had our own swimming pool beyond the playground. That was always our reward for working hard, at the end of a summer afternoon!

4 🔘 02 Play the CD again. Students check their answers in pairs before you check answers as a class.

Answers

1 incorrect
2 incorrect
3 correct

Further practice

Ask students to work in pairs and talk about the different rooms in their school. They should say which ones they like or don't like and why. Monitor as they are working, helping where necessary.

5 Check students understand the words in the exercise. Students work in pairs to complete the exercise. Check answers as a class.

Answers

attend classes each day
work hard
get good grades
wear a uniform every day
play football for the team
go to an after-school club

perform on stage
hand in homework on time
go on school trips
pass exams
eat a packed lunch
arrive late for school

6 🔘 03 Ask students *Do you wear a uniform to school? Do you have to arrive at school on time? Do you have to play games or do gym?* Students listen and find out about Sarah.

Answers

1 incorrect
2 correct
3 incorrect

Recording script

We go to school from 8.00 a.m. to 2.30 p.m. every day, with an hour off at 12.00 when we eat our lunch. We have to attend classes every day unless we're sick, and we have to get good grades if we can. But we don't have to wear a uniform – we can wear our own clothes. We have to hand in homework on time, and our teachers always tell us we should do things outside of school, too – like join an after-school club, or play football. And one very important thing – we mustn't arrive at school late!

7 After the students' discussions in pairs, elicit a few examples from different pairs to write up on the board. Try to elicit a sentence with each verb to write on the board.

Exam task

🔘 04 Read through the Exam tip with the class. Encourage them to use the time they are given in the exam to read through the questions. They should underline important words to help them listen for the correct information.

Answers

1 A Jake says that because it wasn't finished before the summer holidays, *he didn't know what it'd be like*.
2 B Although Holly thinks the old hall was quite old, Jake liked it because of all the people that studied there, so he was *sad when they decided to build a new one*.
3 B Holly thought she'd miss it, but they didn't use it very much anyway, so it's been OK.
4 A Holly says the heating cost a lot to install but *it'll definitely be worth it*.
5 B Jake says he doesn't know if classical music *is really for me*.
6 A Jake will consider it if Holly goes, and *she wouldn't miss it for anything*.

Speaking

Part 1

1 Check students' answers before they ask and answer the questions in pairs. Then as a whole-class activity, give students a question number and get them to choose other class members and ask the questions.

Answers

1 c
2 e
3 h
4 a
5 d
6 g
7 b
8 f

2 Choose students to say the letters. Ask others if they are corrrect. To help them remember the correct pronunciation, ask students to group the letters by sound:
A J   C G B E P   I Y   W

3 🔘 05   Students work in pairs to spell out the names. Then play the CD so they can check their answers. Ask individuals to spell out the names after they have listened. Help students correct each other.

4 🔘 06   Students listen and write down what they hear.

Answers

1 Mr Broadstairs
2 Mrs Pemberton
3 John Faulkener
4 Gary Jessel
5 Jill Mearham
6 Mrs Delahaye

5 Spell out your surname to the class for them to write down. Students work in pairs to write down all the words. Choose a few students to spell out their partner's details to the class.

6 Encourage students to develop their answers to questions in Part One of the Speaking Test, rather than just giving short answers. Remind them that the examiner can only judge their English on what they actually say in the test, so they must speak as much as they can.

Answers

Question	A	B
Do you like English?	Yes	The grammar is difficult, though.
Where do you live?	Italy	In a small town called Chiavari.
Tell us about your English teacher	Her name's Tina.	She's young and friendly, and she makes us laugh.
What do you enjoy doing in the evening?	Watching TV.	My favourite programmes are music shows.
Tell us about your family.	There are three of us.	My mum's a nurse and my dad works in an office.

7 This exercise works on encouraging students to develop their answers as fully as they can, e.g. *I'm from Madrid in Spain. Madrid is the capital of Spain and it's a beautiful city.*

Exam task

🔘 **07** Read the Exam tip with the class. Play the first question and pause the CD. Ask different students to respond. Encourage them to develop their answers as much as possible. Continue with the rest of the questions in the same way. Write up any useful phrases or vocabulary on the board.

Recording script

1 Where are you from?
2 What are you studying?
3 Where do you live?
4 What do you do in your spare time?
5 Tell me about your family.
6 What did you do last Saturday?

Further practice
Write the questions on the board and ask students to work in pairs to ask and answer them.

Grammar

Present simple & present continuous

1 Either ask the students to refer to the Grammar reference on page 78 before they do the exercise or to use it to help them check their answers after they have finished.

Answers
1 routines – things we do every day
2 things that are happening now
3 the present continuous

2 Tell students they should read through the complete text before they start the exercise. Give them three minutes to read it through silently. Tell them not to think about choosing the correct words at this stage – they should only try to understand the gist of the text. Ask them to say what it is about (what Amy is doing at the moment). Students then read it again and make their choices. They can compare their answers with a partner before you check as a class. Choose students to read whole sentences aloud.

Answers
These are the correct forms:
1 I'm sitting
2 watching
3 I watch
4 I get
5 I'm trying
6 I'm writing
7 Mum's cooking
8 she usually makes
9 she never has
10 we're working and studying

3 Monitor as students discuss what is happening in Amy's house now. Then suggest some verbs to help students describe what might be happening now or what happens regularly in their house or school.

sit	watch	cook	read
talk	go	eat	look
listen	visit	meet	wear

Get them to also make some negative sentences, and ask their partner questions, e.g. *What are you doing in the classroom at the moment? I'm not writing a diary. I'm talking to you.* Say *Amy is talking about a Friday evening. What do you usually do then?*

4 Students correct the sentences individually. Before they do the exercise, remind them that we use the present continuous to talk about what is happening now or to talk about a plan for the future. The present simple is used to talk about routines or habits and is used with those verbs which are stative, i.e. cannot be used in the continuous.

Answers
2 plan   3 I want   4 I have   5 I love   6 finishes

See the Workbook and CD ROM for further practice on these tenses.

-ing forms

5 Students decide which words mean *like* and *dislike*, then add the prepositions to the other words. Suggest that they learn the adjective plus preposition combinations.

Answers
Box One
+: like, don't mind, quite like, love, look forward
-: can't stand, dislike
Box Two afraid *of*   interested *in*   look forward *to* worried *about*   fond *of*

6 Point out the verbs used after these words take the *-ing* form or a preposition plus *-ing* form.

Answers
1 going
2 to getting
3 in learning
4 cycling
5 at making
6 about failing

See the Workbook for further practice.

Further practice
Ask students to make sentences about themselves using the verbs.

To give them prompts to talk about, you could write examples like the following on the board or on cards between pairs:

playing football	eating ice cream	getting low marks in class
studying history	going to museums	walking home in the rain
learning to drive	getting up early	arguing with friends
cooking	helping with housework	cleaning my room
getting home late	travelling alone by bus/on a train	remembering my friends' birthdays

Reading

Part 5

1 Get students to look carefully at the sentences in the exercise, as they often find it difficult in a Part Five to fill gaps at the beginning of a sentence. If they find this difficult, look at how the sentence would have to change if the alternative word was used in the sentence, e.g. in number 1 *Although* instead of *Because* (with *Although* we need an opposite idea in one clause, e.g. *Although I enjoy school, I don't look forward to going every day.*). This will help to show the differences.

> **Answer**
> 1 Because
> 2 Unless
> 3 If
> 4 However
> 5 Although
> 6 Despite

2 Students complete the exercise and then compare with a partner. Check answers as a class.

> **Answers**
> 1 Because
> 2 Although
> 3 However
> 4 If

Exam task

Remind students to read through the whole text before beginning to answer the questions. Students work alone to complete the task. Allow them 15 minutes. Check answers as a class.

> **Answers**
> 1 A   2 C   3 D   4 C   5 B   6 D   7 B   8 A   9 D   10 B

3 Students work in pairs to answer the questions. Encourage them to give detailed answers. Monitor as they are speaking, helping where necessary. Ask the class how many of them would like to go to such a school.

4 Discuss as a class. Elicit differences from the class.

CLIL Ask students to do some research into what school was like in the past in their country. It could just be one or two generations back, i.e. parents and grandparents.

Ask them to see what they can find out from the Internet, and also from interviewing people in their family on different aspects of school life then, e.g. how they travelled to school, their classrooms, the subjects they studied, what their teachers were like, and how severe they were. Families may have some old photos of local schools that could be scanned into the computer. Any photos or pieces of writing that the students do can then be made into a wall display, which will be useful for practising use of the past tense, particularly *used to*.

Writing

Part 2 – Notes & emails

1 Ask students to read through the note in pairs first and summarise what they have read, then answer the questions to test their understanding.

> **Answers**
> 1 The note is to Jennie.
> 2 The note is from Samantha.

2 Students now match two of the verbs in the box with the information in the note.

> **Answers**
> apologising, explaining, inviting (The writer is apologising that she couldn't go to the party, explaining why she couldn't go and inviting Jennie to her house.)

3 Students read the note again and extract the correct phrases. You could then ask students to look at page 86 to find out more about this part of the exam.

> **Answers**
> Explaining   I wasn't very well, so I had to stay at home.
> Inviting   Would you like to come ...

4 Using the verbs in Exercise 2, students match them to the sentences.

> **Answers**
> 2 thanking
> 3 advising
> 4 describing
> 5 warning
> 6 suggesting
> 7 apologising
> 8 inviting
> 9 explaining

Further practice

As a follow-up, get each pair of students to write down another example for each of the verbs. They could then read them to another pair, who have to identify which verb it is an example of.

5 Elicit a couple of examples from the class. Then in pairs, they write their own examples. Choose pairs to read their notes aloud.

> **Suggested answers**
>
> A I'm sorry I couldn't meet you yesterday, but unfortunately I fell off my bike on the way to school in the morning and I hurt my leg.
> Would you like to go to the cinema tomorrow? There's a good film on.
> B I went shopping yesterday and I bought a great skateboard with a picture of a lion on it. It's really cool! Let's go to the skatepark at 5.00 today, shall we? Then I can try it out!

Linking words

6 Elicit examples with each linking word to make sure students understand them. Students complete the exercise in pairs. Check answers as a class.

> **Answers**
>
> 2 I arrived home and (I) opened the door.
> 3 I shouted hello but no one was at home.
> 4 I was hungry so I made myself a sandwich.
> 5 My sandwich wasn't very nice because I'd put lots of salt in it.
> 6 I wanted to make toast but I'd used all the bread.

Further practice

Ask students to write some pairs of sentences that need linking words in pairs. Choose pupils to write their sentences on the board and for the class to suggest the linking word.

7 Students work individually to complete the sentences before checking as a class.

> **Answers**
>
> 1 so
> 2 and
> 3 because
> 4 but
> 5 Although
> 6 Despite

Beginnings & endings

8 Go through the phrases pointing out that some phrases you would only use with friends, but some are more formal and could be used to e.g. a teacher. The more formal ones are *Dear Jan* and *Best wishes*. Explain to students that these notes are shorter than the usual length required for Part 2 – they are just practising beginnings and endings of notes here. Get them to think about their answers in pairs before they put anything in writing.

> **Suggested answers**
>
> 1 Dear Mrs Smith,
> I'm sorry but I can't come to class today because I'm sick.
> Best wishes,
> Ben
> 2 Hi Sam,
> I think you borrowed my sunglasses yesterday – could I please have them back?
> Thanks,
> James

Punctuation

9 Read through the Exam tip with the class. Ask them to explain when we use a full stop (at the end of a sentence). Ask *What do we use at the end of a question?* (a question mark). *When do we use a capital letter?* (at the beginning of a sentence and for names)

Ask students to read through the letter first and then add the punctuation. They can check with a partner before you check as a class. Finally, point out the use of commas in this note.

> **Answer**
>
> Hi Robyn,
> I'm sorry, but I can't come to the cinema tomorrow. I have to go to the dentist. I'd forgotten all about it until my mum reminded me. I don't think I'll be home in time for the film. My appointment's at two o'clock and the film starts at three, doesn't it? Maybe we could go on Saturday instead. What do you think? Let me know.
>
> See you soon,
> Jennie.

Exam task

Read through the Exam tip with the students. Then read through the Exam task. Ask students questions (they can imagine the answers):

Where did you buy the poster?
What is it a poster of?
When can I come and see it?

This should help them write a complete answer.

> **Sample answer**
>
> Hi Jan,
> Guess what? I've bought a new poster for my room! I got it in town yesterday.
>
> It shows my favourite rock band performing at a concert – it's really cool! Could you come round tomorrow and see it? That would be great!
>
> See you then,
> Samantha

2 Winning & losing

Unit objectives

PET TOPICS:	sport, hobbies and leisure
GRAMMAR:	review of past simple and past continuous tenses
VOCABULARY:	sports, phrasal verbs with *in*, verb-noun collocations
READING:	Part 3: true/false
	Part 5: choosing the correct words
LISTENING:	Part 3: focus on numbers
WRITING:	Part 3: evaluating a letter, writing a story
SPEAKING:	Part 2: phrases for agreeing and disagreeing

Sport

Reading

Part 3

1 In pairs or small groups, ask students to look at the pictures on page 14 of Olympic sports and name them (swimming, gymnastics, (field) hockey, (synchronised) diving, cycling, running, horse jumping). They should make a list of as many Olympic sports as they can.

Make a list on the board of students' suggestions. Pay attention to pronunciation of the words for sports. Ask students which Olympic sports they enjoy/don't enjoy watching.

> **Possible answers**
>
> athletics, basketball, volleyball, ice skating (winter), sailing, etc.

2 Check students know the meaning of *athlete*, *championship* and *competition* and ask them to complete the table in pairs. Drill the words paying attention to correct word stress.

> **Answers**
>
> 1 champion
> 2 athletics
> 3 competitor
> 4 competitive

3 Ask students to complete the exercise in pairs. Tell them to identify what kind of word is missing. If it is a noun, should it be singular or plural? If it is an adjective, what ending should it have? Remind students what a noun, a verb and an adjective is. Explain that understanding how these word types are used will help them do Part 3 in the exam.

> **Answers**
>
> 1 athletes   2 championship   3 competitive   4 athletic

Exam task

Look at the instructions for Reading Part 3 with the class and the first two sentences. Give the class time to read the

first paragraph of the text. Then ask them to discuss with a partner if sentences one and two are correct/incorrect.

Check the answers with the class and read through the Exam tip together.

> **Answers**
>
> 1A   2 B

Ask the class to read the rest of the text and do the task individually. Students check their answers with a partner. It may be a good idea to pair weak students with strong students so they can provide support. Ask students to identify where in the text the information is given for each sentence.

> **Answers**
>
> 3 B   4 A   5 A   6 A   7 B   8 B   9 A   10 B

4 In pairs, students discuss the questions. Have a class discussion. Check/teach any new vocabulary.

Grammar

Past simple

1 Students work in pairs. If you have a weak class, it may be a good idea to elicit some examples of past simple forms before doing the exercise. Give them a time limit of three or four minutes to complete this task. Then check answers as a class.

> **Answers**
>
> 1 based, started, named, called, helped, attracted, wanted
> 2 began, built, came out, was, had, won, became, grew
> 3 weren't many nationalities; BMX wasn't just about racing
> 4 didn't become

2 In pairs, students choose the answers. Get them to check the Grammar Reference, SB page 79 when they have finished. Check answers as a class. Ask students to explain why the other verbs are wrong.

> **Answers**
>
> 1 like   2 were   3 became   4 won

3 Students do the exercise individually and then compare with a partner. Check the answers with the class. If some students are having difficulty it may be necessary to give them some remedial work on the past simple.

See the Workbook and CD ROM for further practice.

> **Answers**
>
> 1 played   2 didn't/did not learn   3 won   4 did Lauren buy
> 5 Was   6 weren't/were not

Past continuous

4 Look at the examples with the class. It may be helpful to draw timelines on the board to illustrate these concepts.

a) ~~~~~ x
b) x ~~~~~ x
c) ~~~~~ x ···············

Answers

a 2   b 1   c 3

5 Elicit the forms of the past continuous: *was/were + ing*, *wasn't/weren't + ing*. Students do the exercise individually and then check their answers with a partner.

Answers

1 Were you going; saw   2 were winning; scored

6 Students take turns asking and answering the questions with a partner. Monitor as they are working, taking note of any mistakes. Choose some pairs to ask and answer a question in front of the class. Go over any mistakes with the class, asking them to try to correct them.

See the Workbook and CD ROM for further practice.

Listening

Part 3

1 🔘 08 Explain that in Listening Part 3 it's often necessary to write down numbers and/or spell names. Ask students to say the numbers aloud before they listen. Highlight any pronunciation difficulties or problems with saying dates. Play the recording.

Students compare answers with a partner. Then elicit the answers from the class.

Recording script and answers

1 the 30th of March
2 It costs £1.15.
3 I was born in 1998.
4 There were 2,500 people there.
5 My parents moved to this house in 2001.

2 🔘 09 This exercise gives students practice in listening to numbers in context. Ask them to read the information about Tyler Wright. Read through the Exam tip with the class and elicit suggestions about what kind of information they will need, e.g. 1 a date, 2 a number, 3 a number, 4 a year, 5 a number less than 20. Then play the recording. Students compare answers before listening again if necessary.

Answers

1 31st March
2 14
3 30,000
4 2009
5 17

Recording script

Tyler Wright was born on the <u>31st of March</u> 1994 in New South Wales, Australia. She started surfing when she was very young and was already competing by the age of 11. When she was <u>14</u>, she was the youngest person to win the women's event at Manly Beach in Australia beating the world champion. The prize for this event was <u>$30,000</u>. Since then Tyler has earned hundreds of thousands of dollars. She won several more competitions in 2008 and became the under-18 champion in <u>2009</u>. Then in 2011 she won the women's World Cup in Hawaii by scoring a little more than <u>17</u> points out of a total of 20. Tyler says she has her two older brothers to thank for teaching her to surf.

3 Pre-teach *talent*, *luck*, *ambition* and then ask students to discuss the questions in small groups. Ask one person in each group to report back to the class on their group's opinions.

Exam task

🔘 10 Look at the listening task with the class. Explain that it's not just numbers/spellings that are tested. Remind the students of the Exam tip and then ask them to identify the kind of information that's missing in the task with a partner.

Go over it as a class before they listen. (1 date, 2 surname, 3 name of a sport, 4 something you have to do in school, 5 something you can train – a noun, 6 something you organise – a noun)

Play the recording twice. Students compare answers before the second recording.

If you anticipate students will find the listening difficult, photocopy the recording script (see page 67) and allow students to read and listen.

Answers

1 22 April   2 Hawkins   3 hockey   4 homework   5 mind
6 time

Recording script

You will hear a man called Don Wood talking about a special sports school on the radio.

For each question, fill in the missing information in the numbered space.

Thanks very much for the opportunity to tell your listeners about the International Sports Academy or ISA in Florida, USA. My name's Don Wood and I'm a senior coach at ISA, one of the best sports schools in the world. We have 500 talented young athletes aged 12 to 18 studying with us from dozens of countries. You can find out if you've got what it takes to join ISA by coming to an interview on <u>April 22</u> when we're going to select possible new students for next year, which begins on September 15th. If you'd like to be there, you can phone my assistant Leo Hawkins that's <u>H–A–W–K–I–N–S</u> on 0998 354678.

The programme at ISA is busy and varied. You can choose one main sport from all the usual sports such as soccer or football, tennis, swimming, and also <u>hockey</u> which you can do from the start of the next school year. As well as doing normal school lessons, you spend ten hours a week practising your main sport after school. Many of our students also spend the weekends at tournaments all over the USA. As well as your training programme we expect you to find time for <u>homework</u>. And if you need extra help with English, we have classes in that too. Students also learn how to perform well in competitions – that means learning to control the <u>mind</u>, as well as making sure they are strong and fit enough to compete.

So life at ISA is really busy. You need to enjoy a challenge and be very organised. But you don't need to worry about how you'll manage being away from home for the first time. Each student has a personal coach who helps them manage their <u>time</u> and talks about any problems they may have.

If you're talented, confident and believe in yourself, give us a call.

4 Students discuss the questions in pairs. Discuss with the class what the advantages/disadvantages of going to a school like this might be.

Vocabulary

1 Explain that it's important to learn phrasal verbs as they are often tested in Part 5. Ask students to work with a partner. You could allow students to check their answers by using an L1 dictionary if available. Remind students to keep a note of new phrasal verbs they came across.

Answers
2 believed in   3 join in   4 get in   5 staying in   6 give in

2 Students look at the two cartoons and say what is happening. Teach *good/bad loser*. Ask them to give you some examples of good or bad losers. Give your own example if they are struggling. Then either pre-teach any unfamiliar vocabulary or let students use dictionaries to check the meaning of words and phrases in the activity. Students work in pairs to complete it. Check answers as a class.

Answers
A: 2, 4, 6, 7, 9
B: 1, 3, 5, 8, 10

3 This exercise practises common collocations for phrases to do with winning/losing. This is often tested in Part 5. It may be useful to encourage students to note down new words/phrases under the topic of *Sport* in a vocabulary notebook. Also remind students that there is a Wordlist on page 95 for this unit which they need to learn.

Students do the exercise individually before checking answers with a partner. Then check answers as a class.

Answers
1 beat   2 won   3 failed   4 defeat   5 achieve   6 succeeded

Further practice
Ask students to write sentences with the verbs which were not used in the exercise.

Hobbies & leisure
Reading
Part 5

1 Ask the class: *Which team games do you play? Do you prefer team games or individual sports like tennis?*

See the CD ROM for further practice.

Answers
Words to be crossed out:
1 reach   2 make   3 enjoy, bring   4 ask

Exam task

This exercise practises collocations with words from the text. Point out that these different collocations have similar meanings but are not exactly the same, e.g. *get/stay fit and healthy.*

Look at the instructions for the task and the Exam tip together. Remind the class to read the whole text before trying to do the task. Students do the task individually and then compare answers with a partner. Check answers as a class. Then ask the class if they agree with the opinions in this text.

Answers
1 B   2 C   3 A   4 D   5 B   6 D   7 A   8 B   9 C   10 B

CLIL   You could ask the class to research an Olympic team sport (team sports on the 2012 Olympics programme included: water polo, football, field hockey, basketball, volleyball and handball. Ice hockey and curling are in the winter Olympics. In the Paralympics there is wheelchair basketball and rugby, sitting volleyball, football and goalball. From 2016, rugby sevens is included and possibly cricket in 2020.). Each group could do a mini-presentation on a different team sport. They could find out when it became an Olympic sport, which country has won the gold medal most frequently, what the rules of the game are, etc. A debate into whether cricket should be able to return in 2020 could also be fun.

Writing
Part 3

1 Look at the instructions for the task together. Check students realise they only have to write the letter or the story, not both. Ask *How many words do you have to write?* (100) *Can it be slightly more than 100?* (Yes – or slightly less)

2 Ask students to look at the example letter in Exercise 3 and work through the questions with a partner. They should ignore any mistakes in the letter for now.

Answers
1 Yes   2 Yes (past and future)   3 Yes (*First, but, After, and*)
4 Yes (*final, friendly, special, big, good*)   5 Start is fine; *Write back soon* might be a gentler ending;   6 Length is fine.
7 There are no paragraphs. They could be between *there. We; friendly. After.*

3 Explain that Frankie's letter is a good PET answer and point out that they are not expected to write perfect English at PET but that they get extra marks for accuracy. Then get them to try and correct Frankie's mistakes individually before comparing with a partner.

Answers

1 great/good fun   2 scored/got   3 were

4 Ask students to look at the story task again. Get them to think about the ideas to help plan their story. Discuss them as a class. Look at the Exam tip with the class. Elicit some suggestions from them on how to end the story.

You can also refer students to the Writing file, SB page 88.

Exam task

Students write their story in class or for homework. When they have finished it, tell them to look at the points in Exercise 2 and check they have followed them all.

Sample answer

When I woke up, I was very nervous because I wanted to win the competition so much. When I arrived at the swimming pool, I got changed and waited for my race. It felt like hours and hours.

Then it was my turn. Suddenly, I felt calm. 'It's only a race,' I said to myself. I dived in. It was a perfect dive. Everything felt right as I started to swim. I was enjoying myself. I forgot about the competition until the last second. Then it was over. I looked up and saw that my opponents were all behind me. I was the winner!

Speaking

Part 2

1 Explain to the class that in this part of the test they have to discuss something with their partner. They will need to give their own opinions and respond to their partner's opinions, which will involve agreeing/disagreeing. They will need to listen carefully to what their partner is saying in order to respond correctly. In pairs, students read the phrases and put them under the correct heading.

Answers

Agreeing: You're right., That's true., I think so too., I suppose so.
Disagreeing: I'm not sure about that., You're wrong., Yes, but don't you think …?

2 11 Tell the class they will hear two students talking about homework. The first time they listen they should decide whose opinion they agree with, Lina or Max. Then they listen again and tick the expressions in Exercise 1 they hear.

Answers

Expressions used: I'm not sure about that.   I suppose so.
Yes, but don't you think ...   That's true.

Recording script

| Lina: | I don't think we get enough homework. Do you Max? |
| Max: | I'm not sure about that, Lina. I spend about two hours doing homework every day. I think that's enough. |

Lina:	I suppose so. But what about at weekends? I often don't get any. I think other schools get more homework than us and they get better exam results.
Max:	Yes, but don't you think it's important to have time for hobbies and sports?
Lina:	That's true. But most students just watch TV and play computer games. That's just a waste of time.

3 In pairs, students practise agreeing and disagreeing with the statements. If time, the discussion could be broadened to a whole class discussion. Remind them to use the expressions in Exercise 1. Ask students to write out the expressions on a piece of paper and tick the expressions every time their partner uses one of them. Ask students to count the ticks at the end to find out who used the expressions most.

Exam task

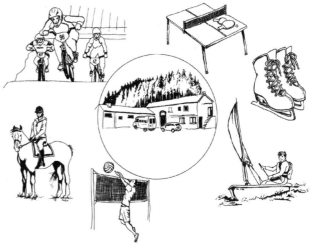

 12 Play the instructions to the class. Ask them *Do you need to talk about each picture?* (Yes) *Do you have to find more than one activity that students would not like to do?* (No) Read through the Exam tip with the students before they do the task in pairs. Remind them that they have to have a conversation so *both* of them have to speak. Monitor as they are working, noting down any errors. Give feedback on the use of phrases for agreeing and disagreeing. Correct any pronunciation errors.

Get the class to repeat the exercise with a different partner.

Recording script

Your school is organising a visit to a large sports activity centre. Talk together about which activities students would most like to try, then decide which activity students would not like to do on this visit.

Further practice

Divide the class into six groups. Give each of them one of the sports from the Exam task. Each group creates a word web for each sport. Allow them to use dictionaries. They can write on large pieces of paper and then present their webs to the class. Then pin them to the classroom wall so that all students have an opportunity to look at them.

3 Let's shop!

Unit objectives

PET TOPICS	shopping and clothes
GRAMMAR	comparatives and superlatives, pronouns, order of adjectives
VOCABULARY	words to describe clothes and shops
READING	Part 1: signs, notices and emails
	Part 5: gap-filling
WRITING	Part 3: a letter and an email
LISTENING	Part 2: multiple-choice questions
SPEAKING	Part 4: talking together about opinions and preferences

Clothes

Listening

Part 2

1 Let students work in pairs to try and describe the clothes. Give them three or four minutes to do this and then go over the answers as a class. Then ask them to describe their own clothes, even if they're in school uniform. Monitor as they are speaking. Ask some students to give descriptions. Go over any mistakes you heard.

> See the Workbook for further practice on the order of adjectives.

Suggested answers:

A a black leather jacket
B a light blue dress with stripes / a light blue, striped dress
C a long orange cotton skirt with pink spots / a long, orange, spotty, cotton skirt

2 Get students to work in pairs. First check that they are familiar with all the words in the 'cloud', then ask them to put the different items in the 'cloud' into the correct categories. Write up answers on the board – are there any items that students don't agree about?

> See the Workbook and CD ROM for further practice.

Answers

Clothes and shoes: jacket, top, sandals, trainers, suit, sweatshirt, gloves, skirt, shirt, jeans, dress
Jewellery: necklace, earrings, bracelet, ring
Colours and patterns: pink, plain, stripes, spots, light blue, gold, cream, dark green, purple, silver, navy blue
Materials: leather, gold, silk, cotton, silver, wool

3 🔘 13 Get students to focus on the points they have to listen for. Play the recording. Students compare their answers. Then ask them to explain their answers by recalling what Marcia said about each thing.

Answers

the department store	✓ (it was their favourite store)
the purple T-shirt with silver stars	✓ (it looked great)
the black cotton jeans	✗ (she wasn't sure about them, and knew as soon as she tried them that they didn't fit)
the silver bracelet	✗ (Marcia didn't like it, but her friend did)
the navy blue sandals	✓ (they fitted her perfectly)

Recording script

Last Saturday my friend and I went into town. I had some money from my birthday, so I was looking forward to spending it! We set off early as we knew it would be crowded later. First we went into <u>our favourite department store</u> and went to try on some jeans and T-shirts. One T-shirt that I tried on was purple with silver stars. <u>It looked great</u>, so I got that. I wasn't sure about the black cotton jeans that I'd chosen, though. <u>As soon as I put them on, I knew they didn't fit</u>. But my friend decided to get <u>a silver bracelet from there. I wasn't keen on it, but she loved it!</u> Then we went into a smaller shop that sold shoes and bags. I found some <u>cool navy blue sandals that fitted me perfectly</u>, but when I took them off, I saw the price – really expensive! Then I looked at some cheaper ones, but I didn't see any I liked – in fact, there wasn't much there for people our age. So we just came home with the things we'd already bought, which we were really pleased with.

---

4 🔘 13 Ask students to read through the two questions and the options. Play the recording again. Get students to listen carefully for the cues to show them they are moving onto the second question – 'Then we went into a smaller shop that sold shoes'. Ask them what they heard that told them to move on to the second question. This is very important when they begin the exam task.

Answers

1 C (they bought a T-shirt and a bracelet)
2 B (there wasn't much there for people their age)

Remind students that the words they see in the options may not be exactly the same as what they hear in the recording, e.g. in the example they've just listened to.

Exam task

🔘 14 Give students time to read through the questions and options quickly before they listen. Ask them to briefly summarise with a partner what they think the recording is going to be about. Read through the Exam tip with the students. Play the recording.

When they've finished the task, ask them to compare answers in pairs and then briefly explain why they put each answer.

Recording script

You will hear an interview with two young teenagers, Ben Wright and Sophie Carter, who design and make their own clothes. For each question, choose the correct answer A, B or C.

Interviewer: Today I'm with two teenagers, Ben Wright and Sophie Carter, who both design and make clothes. Ben, you design your own T-shirts. What gave you the idea?

Ben: Well, my grandma knew I loved art, so for my birthday she gave me some plain T-shirts, with special pens for drawing designs on them. But I didn't really use them until one day when <u>I was watching my favourite rock star on TV. He was playing at a concert in a T-shirt he'd designed himself.</u> So that made me get my T-shirts and pens out again. I looked on the Internet for ideas, and started experimenting!

Interviewer: So how did you put your designs onto your T-shirt?

Ben: Well, I tried drawing them straight onto the T-shirt, but that didn't work very well as my designs were really complicated. Then I found out you can buy special paper that'll transfer your designs onto T-shirts if <u>you iron over the top of it. It was great</u>, as I was worried I might have to sew them on, and I'm not very good at that!

Interviewer: And what did your school friends think of your T-shirts?

Ben: Well, I didn't think they'd like them, but in fact <u>they immediately started getting some designs together and asking me how to produce the T-shirts</u>. They did some really good ones, and we took a photo of us all wearing them. There was even an article about us in the school magazine!

Interviewer: Great! Now turning to you, Sophie. You've made dresses for school parties, haven't you?

Sophie: That's right. Our school started an after-school class with a teacher who designs and makes clothes professionally. The classes are really popular – there are boys and girls of all ages in the school, including older students who'll soon be leaving. <u>Some class members' parents come in too</u>, as the class has got quite big for one teacher to handle.

Interviewer: So why do so many people come to the class?

Sophie: Well, making your own clothes is cheaper than buying them, especially dresses, but the main thing is <u>that no one else will be wearing the same as you at a school party</u>! I like letting other students see what I've achieved too, though! Some students actually think I've bought the dresses I've made!

Interviewer: So what will you do next, Sophie?

Sophie: Well, I've still got lots to learn about sewing, but I really enjoy designing too. <u>I'd like to get better at doing the drawings I need for that</u>. I'm pleased with the colours and materials I've chosen for my dresses, though – they've worked well.

Interviewer: Well, good luck, Sophie and Ben!

CLIL After students have done the Exam task, encourage them to try watching a video clip on YouTube about designing their own T-shirts. They look on www.youtube.com or they can search for a suitable clip on 'design your own T-shirt youtube'.

Students could also collect pictures and information about different fashion designers. Ask them to think about which international designers they know. Which designers are there in their country? If they can put together some photos, they can talk about which styles they like and dislike, and what their personal tastes in clothes are. In groups, they could also put together the information for a short powerpoint presentation for their class.

Speaking

Part 4

1 In pairs, students describe what the teenagers are wearing. Monitor as they are speaking, helping where necessary. Write any new vocabulary up on the board. Ask the class what they think of the clothes and whether they would dress like that or not.

2 Choose students to read the sentences in the speech bubbles. Ask others to put their hands up if the sentence applies to them. Then ask students to work in pairs and discuss where they get their clothes from. Ask a few students to tell the rest of the class about their partner.

3 🔊 **15** Before the students listen to the conversation, get them to speculate first about what could fill the gaps in pairs. They can write a separate list. Students then listen to the recording and complete the conversation. They can then compare the answers before they listened to see if they were correct.

Answers

1 like doing 2 ever 3 How about you 4 isn't it 5 I agree
6 don't they 7 You're right 8 prefer 9 Do 10 ever do that
11 often go 12 Do you think so 13 not sure

Exam task

Read through the Exam tip with the class. Remind them that they need to have a conversation with their partner in the exam lasting three or four minutes. Therefore, a good way of extending the conversation is to ask questions.

Ask the students to work in pairs and do the task. Time them and see which pairs can keep going for three minutes.

Try to monitor and note down any mistakes they make so you can go over any problem areas.

CLIL Ask students to do a class survey about the big clothes shops in their town or city. Which ones do they like? Ask them to collect information about e.g. styles of clothes, prices, what the shop is like inside, and the staff. They could put the results on a graph to compare results.

Shopping

Grammar

Comparing

1 Describe your favourite shop to the students, using the prompts in the box. Suggest some possible answers to the points in the box:

What it sells: what kind of clothes

The prices: high, low, reasonable, cheap, expensive

The size: huge, enormous, small

The staff: helpful, polite, friendly

Students choose their favourite shop.

2 Put students into pairs to talk about their favourite clothes shop, giving reasons for their choice.

3 Remind students about the spelling. Ask *Which adjectives double the middle letter when -er is added?*

Answers

cheap	cheaper	the cheapest
expensive	more expensive	the most expensive
fashionable	more fashionable	the most fashionable
interesting	more interesting	the most interesting
big	bigger	the biggest
comfortable	more comfortable	the most comfortable
good	better	the best
bad	worse	the worst

4 🔘 16 Ask students to read through the list. Tell them to listen carefully to the recording and tick the boxes before they look at Exercise 5 below. When they've completed the listening, students compare their answers. Check as a class.

Answers

	Denhams	Bryants
cheap		✓
big sizes available	✓	
fashionable clothes		✓
comfortable changing rooms		✓
good sports clothes	✓	
nice food in the café	✓	

5 Students use the information to complete the exercise individually. They check their answers with a partner before you check as a class.

Answers

1 cheaper
2 bigger, than
3 as, as
4 more comfortable
5 better, than
6 as, as

6 🔘 17 Give students two minutes, working in pairs, to come up with possible words to complete both sentences. Play the recording for students to check which answers are correct.

Answers

1 the most interesting
2 the best

Recording script

There's a really big department store in my city, too, called Cavenhams. They sell the most interesting books in the city, I think, and their milkshakes are definitely the best anywhere!

7 In pairs, students compare the shop they chose in Exercise 1 with another shop. They take turns giving a sentence comparing the two shops. Monitor as they are working, checking that they are using the comparative forms correctly.

See the Workbook and CD ROM for further practice on comparing.

Further practice

Students could also compare their town with another town they've been to.

Reading

Part 5

Exam task

Get students to read through the whole text quickly before they begin, to see how much they can understand without the gaps filled in. Ask if anyone has ever visited Harrods, and what they already know about the store.

Answers

1 B	6 B
2 D	7 D
3 C	8 A
4 A	9 B
5 C	10 C

CLIL Ask students to do a short research project into a well-known and well-established department store in their town, or their country. How did the store begin? Has it changed a lot since it started? What did it sell when it first opened?

Reading

Part 1

1 Get students to complete the questionnaire individually and then compare answers with a partner. Get them to give reasons for their answers. Encourage them to add further information as they would do in the Speaking test.

2 Encourage students to think where they might see signs and notices around their town and what they might be for, e.g. in the town – don't drop litter, rules about dogs, traffic signs; in a shop – signs about where to pay, what's on each floor, the café, closing times, changing rooms.

3 Ask students to complete the task and then compare their answers with a partner, and to discuss anywhere they disagree.

Answers

at a cash desk A
inside a fast food restaurant E
at a bus stop C
inside a changing room F
on a station platform D
at a cinema G

4 Refer students to the Exam tip. Remind students of the differences between formal and informal language and that it is important that they get the correct tone in their writing. For example, in the formal signs the word 'depart' is used; if we were writing a note to a friend, we would say 'leave'. Check answers as a class.

Answers

2 d   3 f   4 c   5 a   6 b

5 Get students to look carefully at the email so that they're clear who it is to and from, and what it is about. Check that they agree about the answers.

Answers

1 The email is to Jane.
2 The email is from Maria.
3 They could be friends, classmates or cousins.
4 The email is about arrangements for a shopping trip on Saturday, and buying a present.
5 There are contractions: *My dad's, he'll, we'll*; there are incomplete sentences: *OK?, – any ideas?*; there's a phrasal verb: *pick up*.
6 giving information, asking for a suggestion

6 Ask students to read the email again and choose the correct answer. Go through why the others are wrong.

Not *A* because Maria asks Jane for suggestions, she doesn't give any.

Not *C* because Maria doesn't ask if Jane is still going shopping; she just says when she'll pick her up.

Answer

B

Exam task

Read through the Exam tip with the class and establish what each notice is doing: 1 telling; 2 telling; 3 telling, suggesting; 4 telling; 5 telling, asking

Tell them to read each notice carefully before they read each choice. Students work individually to complete the exercise. Check answers as a class.

Answers

1 B   (the shop doesn't give refunds)
2 A   (Jake and Dan won't be in the café after 3 p.m.)
3 A   (there's just been a delivery so students can buy items)
4 B   (a maximum of three items only is allowed)
5 C   (Harry wants to know which shop Dan bought them from)

Writing

Part 3

1 Read through the Exam tip with the class. Encourage them to keep a list of things they should check when they are reading through their pieces of writing, e.g. do they always write *then* rather than *than*?; do they know the rule about doubling letters in comparative adjectives?, etc.

Ask students to describe and compare the two photos, using the words in the box, e.g. *The girl is fashionable and stylish. She is wearing comfortable clothes. She isn't wearing traditional clothes. The boy is casual but smart. He is wearing fashionable clothes.* Ask whether the teenagers in the photos are dressed in a similar way to how they themselves might dress.

Refer students to the Writing file, page 88.

2 Ask the students to work in pairs to answer the questions. Choose some pairs to give the class their views.

3 Students read the description in pairs and decide how it relates to the place where they live. Elicit from the class what they think is fashionable in their town at the moment.

4 Put the following example on the board: *I wanted to visit the new store, but then I found out <u>the new store</u> isn't open yet.* Ask students what could replace the underlined words, and why this is important. (*it* – We use pronouns so we don't need to repeat things in sentences).

Students answer the questions in pairs. Check answers as a class.

> **Answers**
> 1 a 2 b 3 a

5 Ask students to read out the two versions of the first sentence (before and after adding pronouns), to compare the differences. Do they think the one with pronouns sounds better? Why?

Students complete the exercise in pairs. Check answers as a class.

> **Answers**
> 2 She 3 them 4 they 5 It 6 there 7 his 8 he
> 9 we 10 that 11 us

6 Read the Exam tip about *which, where* and *who*. Why do we use these words? (to link sentences so that we don't need to repeat things). Students find examples of sentences with *which, where* and *who*. Refer students to the Grammar reference, SB page 80.

> **Answers**
> I also go shopping in my favourite shop, <u>where</u> I can get things like jewellery cheaply.
> My older sister doesn't mind if I borrow the clothes, <u>which</u> is lucky
> ... then my dad leaves me to meet my friends, <u>who</u> love shopping in town, too ...

7 Ask students to read the sentences and underline the words that are cut in the second sentences. What are they replaced by?
a: She – who; b: there – where; c: It – which

Ask students to work individually to write complete sentences. Remind them of the examples where they looked at words to cut.

> **Answers**
> 1 I go to a small shop near the market where you can buy great clothes.
> 2 I bought a really pretty dress, which was quite like one of Isabelle's.
> 3 I showed the dress to Isabelle, who thought it suited me.
> 4 My sister liked my dress too, which surprised me/which was a surprise.
> 5 Then yesterday I saw one of my classmates who was wearing the same dress!
> 6 Next week we're going shopping together, which will be fun.

8 In pairs, students discuss the exercise. Remind them that they are crossing out the word that is wrong. Check answers as a class.

> **Answers**
> Words to cross out:
> 1 who 2 which 3 who 4 which 5 which 6 who
> 7 who 8 who

> See the Workbook for further practice.

Exam task

Before they begin the tasks, students could be encouraged to make brief notes on both questions to think about what they could write. In the exam, they only have to choose one, but they need to make sure they choose the one that they can write more about.

Ask them to compare their notes for each one and say which one they would choose if they had to select only one.

> **Sample answers**
> 1
>
> Hi Becky!
>
> Thanks for your letter. It was great to hear from you.
>
> Let me tell you about the clothes I like wearing. I usually wear quite smart, casual clothes, like jeans and nice T-shirts. When I go out, I prefer to wear a dress if it's not too cold.
>
> I don't really like school uniforms, so I'm happy that we don't wear them at my school. I like choosing my own colourful clothes, and uniforms are usually in really dark colours. I hate sweatshirts, too – at my brother's school they have to wear them every day.
>
> Hope that helps, and good luck with your project!
>
> Best wishes,
>
> 2
>
> Sarah was excited about her fantastic costume as she set off to the party. Sarah had made it herself, because she wanted to look like her favourite pop star. When Sarah arrived, all her friends were already there. Most of them were dressed as monsters or animals, so they were amazed when they saw Sarah!
>
> But when she started to dance, her high shoes really hurt her feet, so she had to sit down. She was just thinking she should go home when she heard a voice, 'And first prize for tonight's best costume goes to ... Sarah!' She had won a beautiful bracelet to wear!

4 Relax!

Unit objectives

PET TOPICS:	entertainment and media, personal feelings, opinions and experiences, hobbies and leisure, free time
GRAMMAR:	present perfect simple, adverbs of indefinite time (*just, yet, already*)
VOCABULARY:	adjectives, prepositions following adjectives, word families
READING:	Part 4: multiple-choice reading comprehension Part 5: thinking about gap-fill options
LISTENING:	Part 1: multiple-choice – matching pictures to questions
WRITING:	Part 1: word building
SPEAKING:	Part 3: *look/looks like*, speculating, paraphrasing, dealing with unknown vocabulary

Personal feelings

Reading

Part 4

1 Elicit some examples of science fiction films, scary movies and comedies before students complete the table. You could give some examples of your favourite films. Students then stand up and walk round the class asking, *Do/Did you like xxx?* as the present perfect hasn't been introduced yet – so avoid *Have you seen xxx?*

As a class round-up, find out which are some of the class's favourite/least favourite films.

2 Students work in pairs to discuss the questions. Write some of the students' facts/opinions/feelings on the board and ask the class to say whether each one is a fact, an opinion or a feeling. Monitor as they work, noting down any mistakes. Go over these when the students have finished the activity.

3 This exercise will raise students' awareness that Part 4 focuses on understanding the opinions, attitudes and feelings expressed in the text.

4 Students work in pairs to discuss the questions.

> **Answers**
> 1 fact   2 feeling   3 fact   4 opinion   5 opinion

Exam task

Look at the instructions and the Exam tip. Then tell the class to read the whole text before trying to answer the questions individually. Students compare answers in pairs.

> **Answers**
> 1 D   2 B   3 C   4 D   5 A

5 Check students' pronunciation of the adjectives. Students find the adjectives in the text. Check answers as a class.

> **Answers**
> worried – anxious, nervous
> fantastic – great, terrific

6 Students work in pairs. Check answers as a class.

> **Answers**
> excited – a   frightening – b   scared – a
> boring – b   frightened – a

7 Ask students to choose the correct adjective individually and complete the sentences. Then compare their answers. Check answers as a class. Elicit answers for each one from a number of students.

> **Answers**
> 1 frightened   2 worrying   3 exciting

8 When students have done Exercise 6, summarise the use of adjective forms on the board. *I am/get ....ed, I think x is ...ing.* Elicit some more adjectives that work this way, e.g. *interesting/interested, boring/bored.*

Students then work in pairs to think of a film to recommend. Monitor as they are working. Ask pairs to join together to recommend their films. Choose some pairs to tell the class their recommendation.

Grammar

Present perfect

1 As a class, elicit the answers to the rules for the use of past simple/present perfect for finished and unfinished time. Check students know how the present perfect is formed. Refer them to the Grammar reference, SB page 81.

> **Answers**
> 1 past simple   2 present perfect

2 Students work in pairs. If students find this tense difficult, it may be worth comparing uses of past forms in their language with the uses of the present perfect in English.

> **Answers**
> 1 very recently   2 is not given

3 In pairs, students complete the exercise. Point out that *never* has a negative meaning but is used with a positive form. Give students an example: *My mother has never watched a scary movie. = My mother hasn't ever watched a scary movie.*

> **Answers**
> 1 Have   2 's/has   3 've/have   4 's/has
> 5 hasn't/has not   6 haven't/have not

4 Students complete the exercise individually and then compare answers with a partner. Elicit examples from different students.

5 Let students work in pairs to complete the exercise. Go over any problem areas as you check answers as a class.

> **Answers**
>
> 1 have been 2 won 3 read 4 has 5 have been

6 Check the word order once students have finished the first part of the exercise. Drill the questions, write prompts for each question on the board and see if students can ask the questions in pairs from memory.

> See the Workbook and CD ROM for further practice on the present perfect.

> **Answers**
>
> 1 How many films have you watched on DVD this week?
> 2 How many times have you been to the cinema this month?
> 3 Have you ever seen a film in another language?
> 4 Which film have you seen more than five times?
> 5 Have you ever cried in a movie?
> 6 What's the scariest film you have ever seen?

Further practice

Students think of one or two more questions to ask each other/the class about films using the present perfect where possible, e.g. *What's the best/worst/funniest/film you have ever seen? Who's your favourite actor/actress? Have you seen all their films?*

Reading

Part 5

1 Check students know the meaning of these adjectives. Practise the pronunciation. Check answers as a class.

> **Answers**
>
> jealous, afraid + *of*
> annoyed, surprised, worried, excited, serious, anxious + *about*
> disappointed, annoyed, surprised, worried, excited + *by*
> disappointed, annoyed, satisfied + *with*

2 Students work in pairs to discuss the questions. Monitor as they are working, noting down any errors to go over at the end of the activity. Students can use some more of the adjectives in Exercise 1 to ask further questions, e.g. *Have you ever been afraid of anything?*

Exam task

Look at the instructions and the Exam Tip together. Tell the class to read the whole text before trying to fill the gaps. Students work individually and then compare answers in pairs. In class feedback, focus on questions which test target language: the present perfect (1 and 2); adjectives + prepositions (7 and 9).

> **Answers**
>
> 1 A 2 D 3 B 4 A 5 D 6 A 7 B 8 B 9 B 10 C

3 Go over the vocabulary for musical instruments. Common instruments to teach include: piano, guitar, drums, flute, trumpet, violin, cello, clarinet, saxophone. Remind them that we use *the* with instruments, e.g. *I can play the piano.* Encourage students to write the list of instruments in their vocabulary notebooks. Students discuss the questions in pairs.

CLIL Students could choose a famous young classical musician to write a mini biography of, e.g. Lang Lang, Brianna Kahane. They could also find out what the benefits of learning a musical instrument are.

Entertainment & media

Listening

Part 1

1 Encourage students to get into the habit of identifying things in the pictures in Part 1 during the preparation time before they listen. It will focus their attention on the information they need to understand. Go over ways of saying the time, e.g. *seven fifteen; a quarter past seven*, and the way we talk about money, e.g. *twelve pounds fifty* (£12.50).

2 Training students to do this activity is also vital for success in Part 1 because all the items in the pictures are likely to be mentioned but only one option will actually answer the question.

Exam task

18 Students listen and then check with a partner before the second listening. With a weak class it's worth photocopying the recording script (see page 68) and allowing them to read and listen a third time.

> **Answers**
>
> 1 C 2 B 3 B 4 A 5 C 6 B 7 A

> **Recording script**
>
> *There are seven questions in this part. For each question, there are three pictures and a short recording. For each question, choose the correct answer A, B or C.*
>
> 1   *What time does the film start?*
>
> Boy: What time does the film start this evening, Mum?
>
> Mum: Not until <u>quarter to eight</u>. I thought it started at quarter past seven but that was another film. Anyway we need to be at the cinema by half past seven because there's always a queue to collect the tickets and get drinks.
>
> Boy: So, we won't need to leave here until seven fifteen then.
>
> Mum: No. That should give us plenty of time.
>
> 2   *What did Jenny buy at the film festival?*
>
> Boy: Did you get that T-shirt at the film festival Jenny?
>
> Jenny: I've had this one for ages actually. There were loads of really cool T-shirts there but all much too expensive. The only thing I could afford was <u>a poster</u> but I haven't put it up on my wall yet.
>
> Boy: Did you get any famous actors to sign it?
>
> Girl: No, unfortunately. I wanted to but they were only signing copies of their books.

3	*Which instrument has the boy recently started learning?*
Woman:	So Jack, how are you getting on with your music lessons?
Jack:	Well, I'm finding the violin quite hard at the moment. It was easy to begin with but now I've got to a higher level, it's much more challenging.
Woman:	And you're also studying the trumpet, right?
Jack:	That's what I wanted to learn but there wasn't a teacher available so I took up the flute a few months ago instead. I'm enjoying it and I really like my teacher.
4	*How did the family travel to the concert?*
Woman:	Did I tell you we almost missed the concert? I told everyone to be ready really early because I was worried about the traffic. So everyone was in the car and guess what? It wouldn't start. I couldn't believe it. There wasn't a bus until the following day and the train only went as far as Lipton and then you had to go by taxi. There were no hire cars available either so in the end our very kind neighbour lent us his and we just got there in time.
5	*Which circus tickets did the man decide to buy?*
Man:	There wasn't much choice of circus tickets. There weren't enough of the £12.50 seats for all of us, which is what I was planning to buy. And although there were lots of seats at £14.95, these were only on weekday afternoons, which I know wasn't an option for us. So I'm afraid I've gone for the ones at £17.00. I know it's more than we wanted to pay, but at least we won't be right at the back.
6	*What do the speakers decide to watch on TV?*
Granddad:	There's an interesting documentary about sharks on in half an hour.
Girl:	I think I've already seen it, Granddad. It's really good. I don't mind watching it again. But don't you want to watch the football?
Granddad:	It's not on until very late. I may be too tired to watch it.
Girl:	The Lenny Adams show is on at 9.00. He's very funny. You like him too, don't you?
Granddad:	Umm, I'd rather watch the documentary if you're sure you don't mind seeing it again.
Girl:	No that's fine, Granddad.
7	*Who do the speakers think will win the singing competition?*
Girl:	Who do you think will win the singing competition?
Boy:	I think the one with short dark hair is best.
Girl:	Do you? I think the tall one with the long curly hair has a much better voice.
Boy:	But he sang a really boring song – and he can't dance.
Girl:	That's true. I expect you're right. The others weren't very good, were they?
Boy:	Especially the one with blond hair. He's really annoying. He doesn't have a chance.
Girl:	I agree. But he tried really hard.

Speaking

Part 3

1 🔘 **19** Ask students to give some sentences describing other students in the class. They should talk about their clothes, their appearance and what they are doing. Explain that *look* is followed by an adjective and *look like* is followed by a noun e.g. *He looks funny. She looks beautiful. He looks like a famous actor. She looks like a model.* Students listen to Marco doing the Exam task. Discuss the answers as a class.

> **Answers**
> 1 C

> **Recording script**
>
> The people in the picture look very excited. I think they're waiting for a famous actor. It looks like a special day ... when ... I don't know the word ... the first time a film is shown and all the stars come to see it. Some of the people are shouting and waving ...

2 Elicit the answer from the students, playing the recording again if necessary. Give the students some words in their own language that they didn't know the English for. Ask them to explain them as simply as possible, e.g. *a kettle – this is something that makes water hot.* Other words could be a stapler, a golf tee, a bandage.

> **Answer**
> It looks like a special day ... when ... I don't know the word ... the first time a film is shown and all the stars come to see it. (It's a premiere)

3 Ask students to complete the sentences without listening again.

> **Answers**
> 1 look   2 looks like

4 Students complete the sentences with the correct form of the verb and then check their answers in pairs. Check answers as a class, asking students to read the complete sentences aloud.

> **Answers**
> 1 can see   2 is   3 is playing   4 was taken   5 are walking
> 6 is wearing   7 is   8 looks

Exam task

Look at the instructions and Exam tip before students do the task in pairs. When they have finished, elicit descriptions from the students to build a model answer.

Writing

Part 1

1 Teach the names of the rides in the pictures, e.g. *big wheel*, *rollercoaster*, before students discuss the questions. Ask them if they enjoy going to places like this and if there are any near their home. Students discuss the questions in small groups. Monitor as they are working, helping where necessary. A representative from some groups could tell the class what they discussed.

2 🔘 20 Students listen and write the missing information. This gives extra practice for Listening Part 3.

> **Answers**
>
> 1 castle   2 4/four million   3 48   4 6 p.m.

> **Recording script**
>
> Europa Park in Germany is probably the biggest theme park in Europe. It's been open since 1975, so it's also one of the oldest. The Mack family, who still partly own Europa Park, built the hotel on the site of a <u>castle</u> which dates back to 1442. The majority of visitors are from Germany, but large numbers of people also visit from other countries in Europe such as France and Switzerland. The park attracts over <u>four million</u> visitors every year.
>
> Europa Park has a huge range of rides to suit all ages – from pirate ships to the highest rollercoaster in Europe. There are now <u>48</u> rides in total – more than enough for a two-day visit.
>
> The best time to visit is in summer when the weather is better, but it can get busy during the holiday season. Apart from a few special events, Europa Park isn't open during the winter but you can visit from April to November when the park is open from 9.00 a.m. to <u>6.00 p.m</u>. For more information you can go to the website at ... [fade]

just/yet/already

3 This exercise and the next one give students practice of adverbs commonly used with the present perfect. These adverbs are often targeted in Writing Part 1. Students work individually and then compare answers with a partner.

Refer students to the Grammar reference, SB page 81.

> **Answers**
>
> 1 just – a   2 already – b   3 yet – c, d

4 Check answers as a class when the students have finished discussing in pairs. Then ask the class to write personalised sentences with *just*, *yet* or *already*

> **Answers**
>
> 1 yet   2 already   3 just   4 for   5 never   6 since

5 Elicit the noun and verb forms of the adjectives. Pay attention to the pronunciation, especially the word stress.

> **Answers**
>
> excitement; to excite
> worry; to worry
> enjoyment; to enjoy
> relaxation; to relax
> organisation/organiser; to organise
> challenge/challenger; to challenge
> disappointment; to disappoint
> entertainment; to entertain

Ask which of these words are people. *What do the words end in*? Point out that *-er* often indicates a person and elicit more examples, e.g. *teacher, writer, driver, banker, lawyer, singer, football player.*

6 Students work in pairs to complete the exercise. They can check their answers with another pair before you check the answers as a class. Ask students to tell you the parts of speech (answers in brackets).

> **Answers**
>
> 1 exciting (adj)   2 relaxed (adj)   3 entertainment (n)
> 4 enjoyment (n)   5 worried (adj)   6 challenge (n)
> 7 disappointed (adj)   8 organisation (n)

7 This exercise helps prepare students for the Exam task. It shows how different structures/word forms can be used to give a similar meaning.

> **Answers**
>
> Sentences with a similar meaning: 2, 3, 4, 5
> Sentences with a different meaning: 1 - Sentence **a** tells you there are scary rides at Europa Park but doesn't compare them to anywhere else; **b** compares the rides to others in Germany.

Exam task

Read the instructions and the Exam tip together before students do the task individually. Ask *Can you write two words?* (Yes) *Can you write four words?* (No)

Explain that a contraction e.g. *hasn't* counts as two words (*has not*). They can write either *hasn't* or *has not* in the exam.

If students find this difficult, you can give extra support by telling them how many words are missing in each sentence. Refer students to the Writing file, SB page 88.

> **Answers**
>
> 1 first time (that)   2 hasn't/has not been   3 excited
> 4 (really) enjoyed   5 haven't/have not decided

5 Extreme diets

Unit objectives

PET TOPICS:	food and drink, daily life, free time
GRAMMAR:	future with *going to, will,* present continuous, talking about predictions, arrangements and intentions, modals: *can* (permission), *must* (obligation), *should* (advice), *could* and *may* (possibility)
VOCABULARY:	food and drink, phrasal verbs with *go*
READING:	Part 1: matching words and notices; thinking about who the information is for Part 5: phrasal verbs
WRITING:	Part 2: phrases for suggesting, offering, requesting
LISTENING:	Part 3: thinking about the correct word
SPEAKING:	Part 1: expressing preferences, likes and dislikes

Food and drink

Vocabulary

1 Ask students to look at the photos and ask *Would you like to do any of these activities? Why?/Why not?* Students then work in small groups to match the photos and diets. Encourage them to explain their choices. Also encourage them to guess the meaning of unknown food items, e.g. *fried, raw* from the context.

> See the Workbook for further practice.

> **Answers**
> 1 B 2 C 3 A

2 This exercise clarifies the new B1 vocabulary. Ask students *What do you eat that is frozen/raw/fried/boiled?* Help students with any new food vocabulary.

> **Answers**
> 1 c 2 a 3 d 4 b

3 Check students understand *fit* (healthy, strong and able to do physical exercise without getting very tired) and *healthy* (physically strong and not ill). They complete the questions individually. Check answers as a class. Students then work in pairs to ask and answer the questions. Monitor as they are talking, noting any mistakes to go over at the end of the activity. Ask *Which words are negative?* (*unhealthy, unfit*). *How do you know?* (prefix *un*).

> **Answers**
> 1 healthiest 2 health 3 fitness 4 unhealthy 5 unfit 6 fit

4 Students can do this in pairs and then pool their knowledge during feedback. Tell the class to keep a record of all new vocabulary and to learn it. Highlight pronunciation of difficult items, e.g. *salmon* (silent *l*).

> **Answers**
> Fruit: peach, pineapple, strawberry
> Vegetable: cabbage, corn, lettuce, spinach
> Fish: cod, salmon, tuna
> Meat: beef, turkey

5 Students brainstorm extra food words and then compare likes and dislikes with a partner. You could give them the following examples:

A: I like cherries.
B: So do I./Do you? I don't.
A: I don't like bananas.
B: Neither do I./Don't you? I do.

> **Suggested answers**
> Fruit: apple, banana, cherry, raspberry
> Vegetable: carrot, courgette, potato, beans
> Fish: haddock, prawns, mackerel, sardines
> Meat: chicken, lamb, pork

6 Students match the questions and answers with a partner. Encourage students to give extended answers as in the model. Highlight useful phrases, e.g. *I couldn't live without ...*

> **Answers**
> 1 d 2 b 3 a 4 c

Listening

Part 3

1 This exercise gives students practice in dealing with distraction in the text. They complete each sentence with two possible words. Explain that Danny is the jockey in the photo on page 38.

> **Answers**
> 1 2007, 2009
> 2 chips, ice cream
> 3 53, 55
> 4 fried egg, fruit
> 5 shoulder, knee

2 🔘 21 Students listen and circle the correct word in Exercise 1. Remind them that they will hear both answers each time but that only one is correct. They should check with a partner before listening a second time.

> **Answers**
> 1 2007 2 chips 3 55 4 fruit 5 shoulder

> **Recording script**
>
> Being a jockey was always my dream. I started training to be a jockey in 2007 but I didn't take part in a race until 2009. I came last by the way! The hardest thing about being a jockey is having to stay thin. That means I can't eat a lot of things like ice cream – which I don't really like

anyway. Or chips, which are my favourite! I have to take a lot of exercise to stay fit and to keep thin. Today I weigh 55 kilos but before a race I try to get down to 53 kilos. I keep my weight down by eating healthily. I've got used to this, so I don't mind too much. So, for example, I never have a fried egg for breakfast. Just fruit and one slice of toast. People say racing is too dangerous but I love it. I've been injured once or twice though. A couple of years ago I broke my shoulder and two years before that I broke my knee.

3 ◯ **22** Students predict information about Lee Martin (the polar scientist in the photo). Explain that this is a useful thing to do in gap-fill tasks. Write possible answers on the board before they listen and then see if anyone predicted correctly.

Answers

1 four/4 2 lips 3 strong wind 4 raw fish 5 curry

Recording script

I work as a scientist and spend about ten weeks every year in Antarctica. Most of the time we're in the science lab, but we often go on trips to study the ice. The longest I've spent camping on the ice was ten days, but I only did that once. Usually our trips last four days. It's a very beautiful environment, but it can be dangerous. I've seen a lot of people with frozen toes, which is very painful. The worst that's happened to me is getting dry lips – which can get very sore.

We have to eat a lot when we're outside because it's so cold and eating hot food is the best way to stay warm. But sometimes it's hard to cook because the wind is so strong. We eat a lot of high energy biscuits and some of my colleagues eat raw fish, but I hate the taste so I always refuse. We often eat the same thing every day. A lot of soup for example, so it can be a bit boring. What I really look forward to is having a curry at my favourite Indian restaurant. I miss that a lot while I'm away from home.

Exam task

◯ **23** Give students some time to read the task. Ask them to try and guess what kind of information is missing. Students listen and compare with a partner before listening a second time.

With a weak class it may be useful to photocopy the recording script (see page 68) so that students can read and listen to check their answers.

Answers

1 fruit and vegetables 2 eggs 3 Insects 4 hunting
5 a hot rock 6 boil water

Recording script

You will hear a man called Pete Russell giving a talk about an extreme camping trip. For each question, fill in the missing information in the numbered space.

OK everyone. Thanks for coming along to find out about our extreme camping trip. Before I start, can I remind you about the training day? Because it will probably rain tomorrow, we've decided to do this on Saturday instead of Thursday. If you want to come on the trip, you must attend. We're starting at 8.30, so make sure you're there on time.

There are different ways to experience extreme camping, but on our trip it means bringing no food or water with you. We're going to eat only what nature can provide. But don't worry, I'm sure you won't be hungry. We're camping at Sandy River and it's easy to find lots of delicious fruit and vegetables nearby, which you can eat raw. I expect some of these will be quite unfamiliar to you, but your guide will make sure you only eat what's safe.

There are also other types of food you can find. The guide will show you where to look for eggs. There are other places you can look for these apart from trees. For example, some birds leave them in holes in the ground or in the grass like snakes do.

Something that's surprisingly good to eat is insects. These are really good for you and actually very tasty. And I'm not talking about flies and wasps – the ones I'm talking about are much bigger. I promise you'll love them!
Because you really have to be an expert to be successful, one thing you won't have to do on this trip is hunting. You don't want to waste time and end up with nothing to eat.

Now of course we're not bringing any cooking equipment like a camping cooker or a frying pan, so you're going to learn how to cook your food on a hot rock, which is heated underneath by fire. It's a bit slower than using a normal cooker but works surprisingly well.
Now what about drinks? You'll have to live without juices and hot chocolate, I'm afraid. You'll get all the water you need from rivers and streams but you must remember to boil it for at least three minutes to make sure it's safe to drink.
Right, so before I continue, I'll answer any questions you've got about food. By the way there's a very good website which ...

4 Students discuss the question in pairs/small groups. Elicit thoughts from the students to discuss as a class. Ask students to think about where in their country they could go for an extreme camping trip.

Grammar

Future forms

1 ◯ **24** Students listen and write down the missing words and discuss the questions in pairs.

Answers

1 will (he's not certain, it's a prediction)
2 we're starting (yes - decision already made; it's an arrangement)
3 we're going to eat (yes, he wants it to happen; it's his intention)

Recording script

1 It will probably rain tomorrow.
2 We're starting at 8.30.
3 We're going to eat only what nature can provide.

2 Students do the matching exercise in pairs. Look at the Exam tip with the class and perhaps compare future forms in English with students' own language. Refer students to the Grammar reference, SB page 82.

Answers

1b 2c 3a

3 Students do the task individually and then compare with a partner. Check the sentences are correct before students take turns to ask and answer the questions.

Answers

1 are   2 will   3 Are   4 Will   5 are   6 Will   7 will   8 is

4 Ask students to look at the cartoon and explain what is happening. They do the exercise individually. They can refer to the Grammar reference, SB page 82 for help.

Answers

1 you'll love   2 I'm seeing   3 you're having   4 I'll make
5 starts   6 we'll learn

5 Look at the examples with the class and give an example on the board of your own prediction, intention and arrangement for this evening. Students complete the table and then compare with a partner. Do an example with a student using the models in the speech bubbles. Remind them that prediction needs *will*, intention needs *going to* and arrangement needs present continuous.

See the Workbook and CD ROM for further practice.

Further practice

Extend Exercise 5 to a *Find someone who ...* mingling task where students have to find someone who is going to do the same thing at the same time. Using the table they prepared in Exercise 5, they walk round the class trying to find someone who is doing the same as they are.

Health

Reading

Part 1

1 The sentences in this exercise are typical of the information in Part 1 notices. They introduce phrases for expressing permission, obligation, advice, prohibition and lack of necessity. Students work individually and then compare answers with a partner. Encourage students to note down phrases for permission, etc.

Answers

1 c   2 c   3 b   4 c   5 a   6 b   7 b   8 d   9 d   10 a

2 Look at the Exam tip with the class and then ask them to work out where the notices come from. Find out if there are any similar notices in students' classrooms.

Answers

1 B   2 C   3 C   4 B   5 B   6 A/B   7 C   8 A/B/D   9 B   10 B

3 Students choose the correct modal for each notice and then do the rest of the task individually before checking with a partner. Refer students to the Grammer reference, SB page 82.

See the Workbook and CD ROM for further modal practice.

Answers

1 must – a   2 may – b   3 should – b   4 could – a

Exam task

Read the instructions and look at the example with the class. Tell the class to read the information in the texts and options very carefully. Students do the task individually and then compare with a partner.

Answers

1 C   2 B   3 B   4 A   5 C

Reading

Part 5

1 Look at the Exam tip and encourage students to keep a record of phrasal verbs and to learn them. They should do the matching task in pairs. Point out that phrasal verbs are less formal than other verbs with a similar meaning and are used a lot in spoken English.

Answers

1 b   2 d   3 c   4 a

Exam task

Read through the instructions with the class. Tell them to read the whole text before trying to do the task. Students do the task individually and then compare answers with a partner.

Answers

1 C   2 A   3 D   4 B   5 A   6 A   7 D   8 B   9 A   10 C

2 Ask students *Do you eat meat every day? Do you think you eat too much meat? Could you cut down on the amount you eat easily?* Find out what students think of this text and then get them to discuss the questions in pairs.

CLIL Students could do some research into statistics on fast food chains. Each group could choose a different fast food chain. They could find out which ones are most popular in their country. They could focus on what these companies are doing to make their products healthier. Each group could do a mini-presentation on their findings.

Speaking

Part 1

1 **25** Students listen twice to note down the information.

Answers

1 pasta   2 fish   3 go to the beach   4 being a doctor

Recording script

I love food and I'm mad about cooking, so I like most things. I'm always dying for some pasta when I get home from school, so you could say that's one of my favourite foods. Oh and I can't stand fish. That's the only thing I really hate!

I'm really into surfing so <u>I'm hoping to go to the beach this weekend</u>. I usually go with my friends to the beach near where we live. I might go shopping on Sunday but I haven't decided yet.

I don't really know what I want to do as a job. <u>Perhaps I'll become a doctor</u> if I do well in my exams, but I'm not sure yet. I know I want to stay in this town forever. I love it here because all my friends and family are here. There's no way I'll ever leave.

2 Students complete the sentences in pairs and then listen to check their answers. Students practise saying the sentences with the correct stress and intonation.

> **Answers**
>
> 1 mad   2 dying   3 stand   4 into   5 no way

3 When students have put the questions in the correct order, drill them.

> **Answers**
>
> 1 What's your favourite restaurant?
> 2 What are you going to do this weekend?
> 3 Tell me something about your plans for the future.
> 4 What do you enjoy doing after school?
> 5 Do you like cooking?

4 Students read the sentences silently. Then they take turns to ask the questions in Exercise 3 and read the answers aloud. They could then answer the questions for themselves. Encourage them to give extended answers where possible. Monitor and note down any mistakes you hear to revise with the class at the end of the activity.

> **Answers**
>
> A 3   B 5   C 2   D 1   E 4

Exam task

🔘 26 Read through the Exam tip with the students. Play the recording, pausing to give time for students to answer each question in pairs. Give feedback, focusing on any common pronunciation errors.

Students could swap partners and role play the interview using the same or new questions.

> **Recording script**
>
> 1 Where do you usually go on holiday?
> 2 Tell me something about your family.
> 3 What's your favourite subject at school?
> 4 Tell me something about your friends.

Writing

Part 2

1 Students look at the example Exam task and model answer and underline the phrases.

> **Answers**
>
> Offering – I'll provide
> Requesting – Could you bring something to drink?
> Suggesting – Why don't you …?

2 Students identify the mistakes and then decide what the function of each sentence is. They can do this individually and then check with a partner. Encourage them to add to the list. Refer students to the Grammar reference, SB page 82.

> **Answers**
>
> 2 could – suggesting   3 Could – requesting
> 4 Why don't you – suggesting   5 meet – suggesting
> 6 Would you be able to – requesting   7 I'll – offering

3 This gives students practice in proofreading. This is an important skill students need to develop to help them self-correct their written work. Get them to identify the mistakes and then compare with a partner. They can check their answers by using the Grammar reference.

> **Answers**
>
> I will <u>organised</u> → organise   I can <u>to</u> make → I can make
> Will you <u>can</u> be → Will you be   some <u>snack</u> → some snacks
> What about <u>come</u> → What about coming
> we <u>could</u> prepare → we can prepare

Exam task

Read through the task and the Exam tip with the class. With a weak class elicit some of the phrases they could use for suggesting, recommending and offering. Tell students to check they have included all the necessary information and that they have written 35–45 words.

> **Sample answer**
>
> Hi Stefan
> You should definitely go to Pizza Palace. The pizzas are very good and not too expensive. My favourite pizza is the seafood pizza – it's delicious! I can show you where the restaurant is if you like. It's not far from my house.
> See you soon
> Alex

6 My home

Unit objectives

PET TOPICS	house and home, places and buildings
GRAMMAR	*used to,* verbs followed by infinitive or *–ing* form, *do, make, go, have*
VOCABULARY	words to describe buildings, homes, their locations and people who live in them
READING	Part 4: multiple choice Part 5: gap-filling
WRITING	Part 3: a letter and a story
LISTENING	Part 1: multiple-choice questions
SPEAKING	Part 2: discussion about a given situation

House & home

Reading

Part 4

1 Ask students to describe the two photographs. Teach any new vocabulary. Ask a few students *Where would you prefer to live?* Encourage them to give a short comment explaining why. Then students work in pairs to discuss the advantages and disadvantages of living in each place. Ask them to make a list, which they can then compare with the rest of the class.

2 Encourage students to use an English-English dictionary to check any words that they don't know, and record any new words in their vocabulary notebook.

3 Students first work individually and then compare their lists in pairs.

> **Suggested answers**
>
> **weather:** rainy, freezing, snowy, warm, windy
> **your village or town:** cultural events, huge, lively, historical buildings, traditional, peaceful, busy, convenient, crowded, the coast, quiet, in the countryside, friendly, exciting
> **people:** lively, elderly, sociable, smart, quiet, kind, friendly
> **house or apartment:** huge, a garden, a view, cosy, smart, convenient, comfortable, quiet, plenty of space

4 To reinforce some of the vocabulary on this page, ask students in pairs to choose a word and describe it to their partner, who should say the word. This is also a quick and easy way to revise previous vocabulary and can make a good start to lessons.

5 Ask students to read through the text and see how much they can understand without the words filled in. When they've finished, ask them to briefly summarise what they've read with their partner. This helps them to judge for themselves how much they've understood and retained of the text, which is important when doing a Part 4 Reading task.

Students then complete the text with words from Exercise 2. They can check their answers in pairs.

Answers

1 freezing
2 convenient
3 coast
4 peaceful
5 space
6 cosy
7 sociable
8 lively
9 huge
10 smart
11 elderly
12 view

6 ⬤ 27 Play the recording for students to check their answers.

> **Recording script**
>
> I'm from France and I live in a small town near the capital city, Paris. We're in the north of the country, so it can be freezing in winter, but the summers are warm. There are trains that run from my town into the centre of Paris, so it's quite convenient to get there. We can also get to the coast easily if we want to spend time at the beach, although it's quite a long journey.
>
> The house that I live in with my parents and twin brother is in a narrow street in our town. That means there aren't many cars, so it's quiet and peaceful. Inside our house we have plenty of space and I have my own room. It's small but it feels really cosy and comfortable. My parents are very sociable people so we have lots of visitors!
>
> Paris is a lively city with lots to do. My parents love all the cultural events like exhibitions, and I love shopping in the department stores – they're huge, much bigger than the shops in my town! My grandparents live in Paris, in a very smart new apartment. They're quite elderly now, both over 80, so my uncle has an apartment downstairs, just below them so that he can help them, although they're still very independent and like doing things for themselves. From their windows you get an amazing view of the city. I love visiting my grandparents!

7 Ask students to try and remember what attitudes and opinions Bea expresses, e.g. *It's quite convenient to get to Paris by train.; The street she lives in is quiet and peaceful.; There's plenty of space inside her house.; Her room feels really cosy.; Paris is a lively city.; She loves shopping in Paris.; You get an amazing view of the city from her grandparents' window.*

Then students make some notes individually before they begin talking to their partner, using the prompts in the exercise, and the language from the unit as far as possible. They can then turn these notes into a short piece of writing for homework.

> See the Workbook for further vocabulary practice.

Exam task

Read through the Exam tip with the class. Remind students to read through the text quickly to get an idea of what is in it. They should then read the questions and read the text again more carefully to find the answers.

Answers
1 C 2 A 3 B 4 B 5 D

CLIL Ask students to think about any old buildings like windmills or watermills that did important jobs in their area in the past. As an example, show a cross-section of a windmill to see how it worked, grinding corn into flour.

Ask them also to think about the use of horses in their area, and to find any old photos of e.g. well-known streets where people are using horses to get around rather than motorised vehicles. Discuss *When did horses disappear completely? How much were they used on farms? Are they still used now? Are there any areas in their country where horses have to be used as there's little access for cars?*

Grammar

used to

1 Make sure students fully understand *used to* by asking some concept-checking questions and getting them to give some examples of things that they did regularly in the past, but don't do any more, for example, *When I was five, I used to go to bed at 7 o'clock. What time did you use to go to bed?* Elicit answer. Then ask *Do you go to bed at 7 o'clock now? When did you go to bed at 7 o'clock?* Elicit *When I was a baby, I used to go to bed at 7 o'clock.*

Students can complete the exercise and then check their answers with a partner. Refer students to the Grammar reference, SB page 83.

Answers
1 Did you use to
2 didn't use to
3 used to
4 didn't use to
5 Did she use to
6 used to

2 Use the prompts to tell the class about you and then ask a few students a question, e.g. *When I was younger, I used to watch cartoons on TV. I didn't use to watch the News. Did you use to watch the News when you were younger?*

In pairs, students continue. Monitor as they are talking, noting down any errors they make to go over at the end of the activity.

See the Workbook and CD ROM for further practice.

Verbs followed by infinitive / -ing form

3 Students find the sentences. Ask them to look at the Grammar reference, SB page 83. Explain that they need to start learning these combinations and that they should start listing them in their vocabulary notebook. Ask them to complete the table in pairs. Check the anwers as a class.

Answers
Verbs followed by -ing
Verbs followed by infinitive

Check students understand all the verbs. You could give each verb to a pair and ask them to create a sentence (using a dictionary if necessary) to read aloud to the class.

4 Students work in pairs to correct the sentences. Check answers as a class. Point out that if there are verbs + preposition, the verb after the preposition is always –ing. In this exercise, *to* in 3 and *of* in 4 are prepositions.

Answers
1 agree to go
2 like going
3 look forward to seeing
4 consist of going

5 Ask students to complete the exercise individually and then compare answers with a partner. Check answers as a class.

See the Workbook and CD ROM for further practice.

Answers
1 to drive
2 losing
3 breaking
4 to take
5 going
6 to go

do, make, go, have

6 Introduce the exercise by putting up some words and expressions on the board and asking them which verb goes with each one. They can then make some of their own examples before moving on to the exercise. For example:

have *a bath / shower / a good time / problems / fun / lunch*

go *climbing / swimming / shopping / home / out / away*

do *the washing up / well / badly / something wrong / damage*

make *a mistake / a phone call / an appointment / a cake.*

Students discuss the sentences in pairs. Refer students to the Grammar reference, SB page 83 to help them. Check answers as a class.

See the Workbook for further practice.

Answers
1 go 2 do 3 have 4 make 5 do 6 do 7 have

Places and buildings

Reading

Part 5

1 As a lead-in to the topic of the pyramids, get students to talk about some old buildings they might have visited. Are there any in the town where they live? Take some pictures into class of old places in their town / country and encourage them to talk about these places, even if they haven't been there – what do the students know about them?

Exam task

Read through the Exam tip with the class. Remind the students to read the text through ignoring the gaps to begin with. They should try to understand the gist of the text. Students then complete the exercise individually before checking answers with a partner. Check answers as a class and discuss the other options with the students and why they are wrong.

Answers

1 D *offered* is the only one of the four followed directly by *to*
2 C *where* is referring back to a place, Egypt
3 B remind students of previous exercise – *do* your homework
4 A all the nouns go with *in* but only *fact* has the correct meaning
5 B *lives* is for people or animals; *exists* can be used for things
6 D *consists* is the only verb here followed by *of*
7 A remind students of previous grammar – *used to* means it no longer happens
8 B *do* damage to sth – if students don't know this expression, get them to record it in their vocabulary notebooks
9 C *short* only collocates with *distance*
10 C *remind* means help you remember

2 Monitor as students discuss the questions in pairs. Note down any mistakes they make to go over with the class after they have finished. Choose some students to talk about anywhere interesting they have visited.

CLIL Get the students to do some research on the Great Pyramids answering the questions: *Who first opened them and went inside? What did they find there?*

The pyramids are described as one of the Seven Wonders of the World. Ask *What were the others? Where were they? Do they still exist?* Divide the class into seven groups and get them to do a short presentation on one of the Seven Wonders.

Writing

Part 3

1 Get students to imagine somewhere they'd like to visit.

Put up prompts: *I'd really like to go to ...; I've always wanted to go to ...; I'd love to see ...* Elicit ideas from the class.

Then ask them to look at the photos and match them to the names. If possible, take in a world map and show students where the different countries are. Students then ask and answer the questions in pairs. Choose some students to tell the class about their partner.

Answers

1 Buckingham Palace
2 the Taj Mahal
3 the Eiffel Tower
4 the Leaning Tower of Pisa
5 the Great Wall of China

2 Get students to look in pairs at the different locations in the first box and think about why they would / wouldn't like to go there, using the different adjectives in the second box. Get some examples from around the class and write them up on the board, e.g. *I wouldn't like to go to a desert because it is very hot in the day and cold at night. Also I think it is boring because there is nothing to see.*

3 Ask students to read through the email, ignoring the underlined words. Ask them to tell you what it is about. Then look at the categories below the email. Talk about each one, giving an example of each from the email. Ask students to continue the exercise in pairs. Ask *What is each linker doing in the sentence?* Remind students that we use *although* and *despite* in very different ways.

Although it was raining, I went out.

Despite the rain, I went out.

Go over the answers.

Answers

Time links: first, Then, in the evening, After that
Links to explain reason and result: because, so
Links to add a point: also, and
Links to contrast a point: despite, Although, but

4 Using the list of linkers in Exercise 3, students complete the email. When they've completed it, they can read out the completed email to each other. Check answers as a class.

Answers

1 so
2 Although
3 First
4 then
5 because
6 Although
7 and
8 so
9 but
10 because

5 To prepare students for this, write up some sentences on the board, all joined by commas. Elicit from them some sentences about their day – they can also use the linkers they've just practised, e.g. *I get up at 7 o'clock, I have breakfast.* This can change to *I get up at 7 o'clock. I have breakfast.* Or *I get up at 7 o'clock and then I have breakfast.* Read through the Exam tip with the students. Encourage students to read out the sentences. Is there a full stop where they stop? Students write the sentences correctly.

Answers

2 It's going to be great, you can bring sandwiches. – It's going to be great. You can bring sandwiches.
3 Thanks for your letter, it's good to hear from you. – Thanks for your letter. It's good to hear from you.
4 We went to swim in the sea, the day was hot and sunny. – We went to swim in the sea. The day was hot and sunny. / We went to swim in the sea because the day was hot and sunny.
5 A picnic in the park is a good idea, it's very big. – A picnic in the park is a good idea because it's very big. / A picnic in the park is a good idea. It's very big.
6 My mobile rang, it was Sarah, my best friend. – My mobile rang. It was Sarah, my best friend. / My mobile rang and it was Sarah, my best friend.

6 Ask students to try reading the story to each other. Where do they stop – should there be a full stop there? Students insert the punctuation. They read it again. Does it sound all right or have they put full stops in the wrong place? It's a good way for students to check that they haven't written incomplete sentences. (See Recording script for answers.)

7 🔘 28 Students listen to the recording to check their answers. After listening, they add the paragraphs.

Answers

> **Recording script**
>
> We set off early in the morning. The sun was shining and it was hot. We had brought a picnic with us to eat on the beach. We were quite hungry, so we were really looking forward to it.
>
> Finally, we arrived at the beach. The sea was really blue and it was a beautiful day. We got everything out of the car and raced down to the sea. My brother and I got changed and went swimming immediately. Then we ate the picnic. It was delicious!
>
> We spent the whole day on the beach and then came home as the sun went down and it began to get cold. It was a great day!

Exam task

Read through the Exam tip with the class. Ask students to make some notes about the task before they begin, to make sure they have enough ideas to write about. Remind them that they have to make a choice between a letter and a story, so they should choose the one they can write about the most fully. Refer students to the Writing file, SB page 88.

> **Sample answer**
>
> Hi Sam,
> Thanks for your letter. Going to the mountains sounds great. My family and I all love going into the countryside. We last went there on Saturday because the weather was quite nice, although it was raining a bit in the morning. First we prepared a picnic and then got into the car, which my dad drove. We went to a nice place by the river, and had our picnic. Then we walked a long way, until it got cold in the evening. After that, we drove home again. It was a great day!
>
> Best wishes

Listening

Part 1

Exam task

🔘 29 Read through the Exam tip with the class. Ask the students to spend some time reading the questions and looking at the pictures.

Answers

1 B She likes the fact that there's somewhere to go after school and meet friends – in the park.
2 A Her lamp's too big, so she wants to see if there's anything she likes better.
3 A There'll be falls of snow.
4 C The fan was so noisy that he had to switch it off.
5 C The visitor works in a lab doing experiments.
6 B The girl says the tea they had at the café was lovely.
7 A There's a great necklace she's seen and she's going to get that.

> **Recording script**
>
> *There are seven questions in this part. For each question, there are three pictures and a short recording. For each question, choose the correct answer A, B or C.*
>
> *Before we start, here is an example.*
>
> *What do the students agree needs replacing in their school?*
>
> Girl: The head teacher's asked us for ideas on what we think needs replacing in the school.
> Boy: What about an interactive whiteboard for every classroom?
> Girl: Yeah there aren't enough. And everyone loves them, especially the teachers.
> Boy: And that would be better than new computers because everyone has their own laptop.
> Girl: True. And you can use them for everything – you don't need to replace textbooks all the time if you have one of those to look at in the classroom, because you can get digital books.
> Boy: Exactly ... well that was an easy decision.
>
> *Look at the three pictures for question 1 now. Now we are ready to start. Listen carefully. You will hear each recording twice.*
>
> 1 *What does the girl like about her room?*
> Girl: We've just moved to a new town, so I'm still finding my way around – but it's nice. The town we lived in before was bigger and there were some lovely old buildings in the centre, and I quite miss those. But at least there's somewhere I can go after school and meet friends here, in the park. It's usually quiet then and we can walk around. I've heard there's a great shopping mall, too – that's further out of town, though, so I haven't had chance to see it yet.
>
> 2 *What would the girl like to buy?*
> Mum: Your bedroom's looking quite good now, Carolyn. I'm glad we were able to buy that rug in the sales – it looks perfect on your floor!
> Girl: Thanks, Mum – I know what you mean. I'm not sure the lamp is right for my desk, though – it's too big. Could we see if there's anything I like better when we next go shopping?

Mum:	Well, we can have a look when we go to the city centre tomorrow – I still need a new duvet for your brother's bed.
Girl:	OK, good idea.

3 *What will the weather be like at the weekend?*

Weather reporter:	And now on to the weather for Saturday and Sunday – and it's not looking too good, I'm afraid. The showers that we'll see on Friday will die away during the night, but they'll be replaced by <u>falls of snow</u> the following day, as the temperature drops from lunchtime onwards. The good news is that the cold wind that we've had over the past few days won't be with us by the weekend. But the message is still wrap up warm and take an umbrella.

4 *What did the boy dislike about the hotel room he stayed in?*

Girl:	How was your family holiday, Josh?
Boy:	Well, we stayed in a great hotel. My brother and I had our own room next to our parents. It had big, thick curtains that made the room nice and dark in the mornings, so I could sleep late instead of being woken up by the sun, like at home. My brother found it too hot, though, so he kept switching <u>the fan</u> on. It was so noisy – I switched it off once he was asleep! Then I stayed up watching TV quietly.
Girl:	Cool.

5 *Who came to talk to the girl's class at school?*

Mum:	How was school, Brigitte?
Girl:	Great, Mum! A woman came in to give a talk during our science class, and it was really interesting. Our teacher said she's quite famous – <u>she works in a lab in the city, doing all sorts of experiments</u> about how we catch illnesses like colds. I spoke to her afterwards about how I want to be an animal doctor when I'm older, and she was really helpful.
Mum:	Fantastic!

6 *Which drink did they have during their school trip?*

Boy:	The school trip was good yesterday, wasn't it?
Girl:	Yeah – I wish I'd taken more to drink with me on the bus, though. It was quite a hot day, wasn't it?
Boy:	Mmm, and I'd drunk all my orange juice before we even left.
Girl:	Still, it was great to go to that café – <u>the tea</u> they served there was lovely. I think our teacher was quite surprised when we ordered it.
Boy:	I know – she probably expected us to have lemonade like everyone else!

7 *Which birthday present will the girl buy for her sister?*

Girl:	Hi Dad! I'm in town – I'm just trying to find something for Maria's birthday. I know she was hoping you and mum would buy the T-shirt she saw last week, but mum says Auntie Val's got that – so you've bought her a belt instead. Is that right? Anyway, there's a great <u>necklace</u> in one shop I've just seen – I'm sure she'd like it, so I'll get that. Can you pick me up when I've finished shopping? Thanks, Dad!

Speaking

Part 2

1 Remind students that in Part 2, they need to speak to each other about a subject supplied by the examiner. Explain that the phrases in the exercise will be useful. Students work in pairs to categorise them. Check answers as a class.

> **Answers**
>
> **Giving opinions:** I think ... would be more useful.; I'd prefer to take ... rather than ...; I'd rather take ...
> **Making suggestions:** How / What about taking ...?
> **Asking for opinions:** What do you think?; That's a good idea, isn't it?

2 🔊 **30** Ask students to compare their answers, before they listen and check their answers.

> **Answers**
>
> 1 a good idea, isn't it?
> 2 how about taking
> 3 would be more useful
> 4 I'd prefer to take
> 5 rather than

> **Recording script**
>
> | | |
> |---|---|
> | Helen: | Are you all ready for our trip to the museum, Tom? |
> | Tom: | Yes, I've got everything. I've put a guidebook in my bag. |
> | Helen: | That's a good idea, isn't it? And how about taking an umbrella? |
> | Tom: | I think a coat would be more useful. It's going to be cold and windy! |
> | Helen: | OK, well, I'd prefer to take an umbrella, I think, rather than a coat. I might put one in my bag. |
> | Tom: | Fine. |

Exam task

🔊 **31** As preparation, you could ask students to think about what they could use each item for, so that they already have some ideas when they begin their discussion. Read through the Exam tip with the class before they listen to the instructions and begin talking. Time them for three or four minutes as they talk. See if any of them can keep going. Elicit some ideas from the class. Write some useful phrases on the board. Students then change partners and do the activity again.

> **Recording script**
>
> Imagine that you and your partner are preparing for a school coach trip to a castle. Talk together about the different things you could take with you, and then decide which are the most important. Here are some ideas to help you.

7 Wild at heart

Unit objectives

PET TOPICS:	the natural world, environment, free time
GRAMMAR:	past perfect simple, reported speech
VOCABULARY:	animals, the natural world, weather, verb-noun collocations, phrasal verbs with *on*
READING:	Part 5: choosing the correct collocation
	Part 2: matching people and activities
WRITING:	Part 1: focus on transformations with reported speech
LISTENING:	Part 2: using paraphrasing and synonyms
SPEAKING:	Part 3: speculating

The natural world

Vocabulary

1 In pairs, students match the words and pictures. During class feedback, focus on pronunciation.

> **Answers**
>
> 1 gorilla 2 whale 3 spider 4 shark 5 penguin
> 6 elephant 7 bat 8 camel 9 snake 10 parrot

2 Pre-teach any unfamiliar words in this exercise and then let students discuss the questions in pairs.

> **Answers**
>
> 1 gorilla, camel 2 penguin, bat, parrot 3 gorilla, elephant, bat, camel, parrot 4 whale, spider, shark, snake 5 snake
> 6 shark, snake

3 Ask students to complete the sentences with the words in the box. Ask them to read the sentences carefully and decide which part of speech is missing (1 adjective, 2 verb, 3 adjective, 4 noun). They then identify the correct words in the box. They can check their answers using a dictionary. Ask them if they agree with the statements and have a class discussion.

> **Answers**
>
> 1 cruel 2 protect 3 rare 4 wildlife

4 Students work individually and then check their answers in pairs before class feedback.

> **Answers**
>
> 1 E
> 2 a A, C, E b D c B d E e D

5 Students compare their recent experiences at zoos or safari parks in groups. Choose a representative from each group to summarise their thoughts.

> See the Workbook and CD ROM for further vocabulary practice.

Listening

Part 2

1 32 Read the first question with the class before playing the first part of the recording. Students discuss the answers in pairs. Play this part of the recording again if necessary. Go over the supplementary questions.

> **Answers**
>
> 1 A
> 1 All the animals are mentioned.
> 2 The interviewer says *popular*.
> 3 Visitors come especially to see them, more than any other animal.

> **Recording script**
>
> Interviewer: Martin Williams, a zoo keeper from Harland Zoo is here to tell us about the important work being done at the zoo. First of all, Martin, can you tell us what the most popular animal at the zoo is?
>
> Martin: People love our zoo because some of the animals are free to go where they want – obviously not animals which can be dangerous like lions, or animals which could escape easily like monkeys. The penguins aren't shy and they follow people around – that's why visitors come especially to see them, more than any other animal.

2 Students read and underline the key words in the Exam task.

Exam task

 33 Look at the Exam tip and remind the class that paraphrases or synonyms are often used in this part of the test, i.e. they won't necessarily hear the same words on the recording as in the options, A, B and C. (Although the words in the questions are often the same.)

Play the recording twice. Students should check their answers in pairs.

> **Answers**
>
> 2 A 3 C 4 C 5 B 6 B

> **Recording script**
>
> *You will hear an interview with a man called Martin, who works in a zoo.*
>
> *For each question, choose the correct answer A, B or C.*
>
> Interviewer: You've worked at the zoo for 25 years. What changes have you noticed there?

Martin: I joined Harland because it was a very successful zoo. A lot of rare baby animals were born there and it had already moved the bigger animals so they had space to run and play. <u>Since then they've introduced a greater variety of animals</u> – especially birds and monkeys. So it's always changing really.

Interviewer: You obviously love your job – but what's the hardest thing about it?

Martin: People often want to know if I'm scared of working with such dangerous animals, but that's not something I ever worry about. Sometimes <u>I do get a bit tired of cleaning</u> – that's the first thing we do every morning and it takes hours. But at the same time it's great to be at the zoo early in the morning with no one else around.

Interviewer: Some people say zoos are cruel because the animals are bored ...

Martin: Well actually, these days most zoos make a huge effort to keep the animals busy. So, for example, instead of giving them one big meal every day, what we do is <u>put</u> small amounts of <u>food in different places</u> so they actually have to find it. And we keep hiding it in different places so they never know where it'll be.

Interviewer: And I believe you only work with gorillas at the moment. Is that because they're your favourite animals?

Martin: Well, I do love gorillas but that's not the reason. They're very intelligent and they like to form a relationship with zookeepers – so <u>they don't want to see different people every day</u>. They're fantastic. I've learned so much in the last five years.

Interviewer: Have you learned anything surprising about them?

Martin: Well, I knew that they were sociable and lived in big family groups. But I had thought they were always fighting. But they're really quite <u>gentle</u>. I hadn't expected that. They're lovely animals – so generous – always sharing things with each other.

Interviewer: So tell us what's ...

3 Check students understand the meaning of the adjectives in the sentences. Then get them to think of different ways of saying the same thing, working in pairs.

> **Answers**
> 2 something which isn't safe   3 how you feel when you have nothing to do   4 if you have been doing something for a long time, you become experienced at it   5 something you like more than anything else   6 someone who enjoys the company of other people   7 somewhere quiet   8 someone who likes giving things to other people

Grammar

Past perfect

1 Go through the examples with the class and highlight the timeline.

> **Answers**
> 1 before   2 after

2 Students complete the rule individually. They can refer to the Grammar reference, SB page 84. Ask students for some examples of their own about their school, e.g. *The school had built a swimming pool before I started here. I hadn't realised English was so easy until I started learning it at this school!*

> **Answers**
> had; past participle

3 🔘 34 Ask the class to read the sentences and then play the recording. Students check their answers in pairs. Play the recording again if necessary.

> **Answers**
> 1 F   2 F   3 T   4 T

> **Recording**
> Some visitors to City Zoo had a nasty shock yesterday when they came face to face with an adult male tiger. The tiger was <u>found by a mother and her two small children</u> yesterday afternoon. The mother, Elaine Wilson, had gone down to <u>the lake</u> to take a photo when she saw the tiger, who was coming out of the water. She phoned the police and within five minutes they arrived with the zookeeper. The tiger was soon caught and luckily <u>hadn't attacked anyone</u>.
> Zookeeper Eddie Hewson said they weren't sure how the tiger had escaped. None of the tigers at the zoo had ever escaped before. All the cage doors were locked so they think the tiger was somehow able to jump over the fence. They also don't know exactly when the tiger escaped. The last time he was seen was at 8.00 a.m. and he was found at 3.00 p.m., so he was probably missing for at least five hours. The only thing they are sure about is that the tiger definitely wasn't hungry because <u>he'd eaten a large breakfast</u>.

4 🔘 34 Students work in pairs to choose the positive/ negative form of the past perfect. Play the recording again for students to check their answers.

> **Answers**
> 1 had   2 hadn't   3 hadn't   4 hadn't

5 Do the first sentence with the class as an example. Ask *What happened first?* (the tiger escaped) *So which part uses the past perfect?* (the tiger had escaped). Students complete the exercise individually and then compare their answers with a partner.

Answers

1 discovered; had escaped   2 could not go; had seen
3 was; had appeared   4 came; had not studied
5 had never seen; visited   6 went; had not been

6 Ask students to look at the pictures and say what is happening in each one. Look at the example with the class and then elicit the other sentences. You could extend this exercise by asking what other things the class thinks Super Sam had achieved by a very young age. Ask them to write three sentences in pairs.

Answers

b By the age of 10, Sam had sailed around the world.
c By the age of 12, Sam had left university.

7 Students discuss the questions in pairs. Highlight a few of the students' correct and incorrect uses of the past perfect during feedback.

See the Workbook and CD ROM for further practice.

CLIL Students could research some teenagers who have sailed around the world at a very young age, e.g. Laura Dekker, Zac Sunderland, Jessica Watson. They could discuss the advantages and disadvantages of achieving so much at a young age.

Reading
Part 5

1 Check students know the meaning of the words before they do the task. They can use a dictionary if necessary. Read the Exam tip with the class and remind them to keep a record of all new vocabulary including collocations.

Answers

1 avoid, escape
2 cause, give
3 get, provide
4 losing, escaping

2 Explain that three of these phrasal verbs have a similar meaning and then get students to do the task in pairs.

Answers

1 carried on; went on; kept on (continued)   2 passed on (gave)

Exam task

Tell the class to read the whole text before trying to do the task. Point out that they have already practised some of the words in Exercises 1 and 2. Students check their answers in pairs.

Answers

1 C   2 A   3 B   4 A   5 C   6 D   7 C   8 B   9 D   10 C

3 Students do the activity in pairs and then compare answers with another pair or as a whole class.

CLIL You could extend this activity by getting students to do a project on dangerous wild animals from their own country or from around the world. They could focus on the most dangerous insect, fish and animal and make a poster in small groups.

Environment
Reading
Part 2

1 Discuss this question as a whole class. Decide together if litter is a big problem and what can be done about it.

2 Students do the task individually and then compare with a partner. Ask students which words helped them to decide the answers: 1 on the streets, rubbish 2 sea levels, floods 3 run out of 4 local river, hardly any fish.

Answers

1 litter   2 climate change   3 oil   4 pollution

3 Students do the task in pairs. They can add anything else they are worried about. During feedback, find out which statement most students agree with and have a class discussion.

Exam task

Read the Exam task and the Exam tip with the class. Check students understand the word *charity*; elicit some examples of charities from the students. Students do the task individually and then check their answers with a partner. Make sure they are underlining the key information. During feedback, get the class to check that their choice matches exactly what each person requires.

Answers

1 D   2 G   3 C   4 A   5 E

4 Students work in small groups and think of some ideas to help the local environment. Choose a representative from each group to explain their ideas. The class can vote on the best idea.

Speaking
Part 3

1 Students tick the things they can see in the pictures. Check their answers paying attention to pronunciation. Check students understand all the words. If possible, bring in pictures to help explain the other words.

2 Explain that some of the adjectives can be used to describe weather, some the sky and so on. They need to learn which adjectives are appropriate. Elicit the answers with the whole class. Check their understanding of these words by asking concept questions, e.g. *If the sky is clear, are there any clouds? If it's freezing, is it a little bit cold or very cold?*

Answers

1 freezing, humid, mild   2 clear   3 calm, frozen

3 Students complete the sentences individually and then check with a partner. Explain that these phrases will be useful for Part 3 of the Speaking exam.

Answers

1 must   2 like   3 probably   4 sure

Exam task

Read the Exam task and the Exam tip with the class. Then, working in pairs, get students to each describe one of the pictures. Encourage them to use words and phrases from Exercises 1–3.

Monitor as they are working, noting down any mistakes and also phrases and vocabulary used. Go over these at the end of the activity.

4 🔘 **35** Ask students to listen for phrases from Exercises 1–3 in the recording. You could extend this activity by getting students to do the Exam task again with a different partner. They shouldn't describe the same picture again.

> **Recording script**
>
> Boy: I'm not sure but I think this photo was probably taken in Thailand because I know that they have a lot of elephants there. The elephants are having a bath in the river. There seems to be more than one person washing each elephant. Everyone's getting very wet! The men are either standing or sitting on the elephants. I think the water must be too deep for them to stand in. The elephants look like they are having a really good time. I think it must be very hot because the men are all wearing hats and shorts.
>
> Girl: This is a really amazing photo. I think it was taken in Antarctica because this is where penguins live and also the sea has turned into ice so it must be really cold. I think the men must be scientists who've just arrived in Antarctica. They could be living on the ship. They're all wearing the same jackets which look like special jackets for very cold conditions. The penguin is very funny. He looks like he doesn't want the men to take his photo but he doesn't seem afraid of them.

Writing

Part 1

1 Students do the matching task individually and then check with a partner. Read through the Exam tip with the class. Check answers with the class, asking them to explain the changes in the direct statements when they are reported: pronouns change, e.g. *I → She*; verbs go back in time, e.g. *am → was, will → would, had → had had, have you had → had she had*; some verbs do not change e.g. *might have.*

Ask students *When do we use say, tell and ask? Say* is used for a statement, *tell* for an imperative, *ask* for a question.

Refer students to the Grammar reference, SB page 84.

Answers

1 d   2 c   3 f   4 b   5 a   6 e

2 🔘 **36** Tell the class they are going to hear an examiner asking some Part 1 questions. Play the recording twice and ask students to write down the questions.

Answers

Have you always lived in Madrid? Do you like living in the city? Where do you think you will live in the future?

> **Recording script**
>
> Examiner: Have you always lived in Madrid?
>
> Luis: Well, we moved here when I was two but I don't remember living anywhere else.
>
> Examiner: Do you like living in the city?
>
> Luis: Yes, I like living in the city. There are more interesting things to do here. In the country it can be a bit boring.
>
> Examiner: Where do you think you will live in the future?
>
> Luis: I would like to travel. Maybe I'll live in another country for a few years.

3 Students do the task individually and then compare with a partner. Refer students to the Grammer reference, SB page 84.

Answers

1 he had always lived in

2 said he liked living

3 said he might live in another country

4 This gives some extra practice for Speaking Part 1.

Exam task

Read the Exam task and the Exam tip with the class. Students do the task individually and then check their answers with a partner.

Answers

1 don't put   2 have found   3 were used   4 had built
5 are more expensive   6 were interested in

5 Discuss some ideas for recycling plastic bottles with the class.

8 We're off!

Unit objectives

PET TOPICS	transport, travel and holidays,
GRAMMAR	first and second conditional
VOCABULARY	words about ways of travelling, holidays and journeys
READING	Part 3: true/false questions Part 5: gap-filling
WRITING	Part 2: email or note
LISTENING	Part 4: true/false questions
SPEAKING	Part 4: conversation, expressing opinions, likes/dislikes and preferences

Transport

Reading

Part 3

1 Get students to think about the different ways they've travelled and what the advantages and disadvantages are of each one.

   Now get students to do the same with the means of transport shown in the photos, and then give personal opinions about them. How would they feel about travelling by those means?

2 Get students to check that they know all the words in the box. If they don't, encourage them to use an English-English dictionary to check them, and record new words in their vocabulary notebooks. Can they add any more words to the lists for each category? Here are some suggestions: railway line, ferry, public transport, tunnel, van, make a reservation, crew, arrival, cabin, port, route, fare, backpack, travel agent, windscreen. Remind students that we get *on / off* a plane, train or ship; we get *into / out of* a car or taxi.

   > **Answers**
   >
   > **car:** motorway, roundabout, seat belt, speed limit, traffic jam, traffic lights
   > **plane:** airport, boarding card, check in, departure gate, flight attendant, hand luggage, land, pilot, seat belt, security, take off, weigh
   > **train:** crowded, platform, station
   > **ship:** crowded, feel seasick, harbour, rough, security, waves

3 Ask students to explain why they chose their answers. Which words gave them clues?

   Sarah – car   They looked at the map to help dad find his way.

   Mark – plane   The attendant brought him a drink after he'd taken off, and his luggage wasn't too heavy.

   James – ship   He watched big waves outside the window.

4 Students read the information again and choose true or false. Check answers as a class.

> **Answers**
>
> 1 F (They looked at the map to help him find the way.)
> 2 F (His luggage wasn't too heavy.)
> 3 T (He'd expected it to be unpleasant, but it was fine because he took a sickness tablet.)

Exam task

As preparation, get students to read through the text quickly to check what it is about, and ask students to work in pairs and briefly say in their own words what they can remember of the text. Read through the Exam tip with the class and encourage them to underline the correct sections.

Students work individually to do the task and then check their answers in pairs. Check answers as a class.

> **Answers**
>
> 1 B   2 B   3 A   4 B   5 B   6 A   7 A   8 A   9 B   10 A

5 Get students to think about what it would be like inside the submarine, based on their reading. Would they enjoy it, or would they be nervous? Why?

6 Try to give students an example of your own before they do the exercise. After they have discussed in pairs, ask a few students around the room to share their experiences of journeys with the rest of the class.

   CLIL Get students to think of as many words as they can connected with water, e.g. ways of travelling on/in water, different watersports, places where we find water, verbs that describe water and what we do in it.

   Then get students to devise a questionnaire about the different watersports they've done. Were they positive or negative experiences? Why?

   Put results on a bar chart, e.g. *How many people have tried swimming, windsurfing, canoeing, diving. Which is the most popular watersport in the class? Which is the least popular?*

Grammar

First & second conditionals

1 Read through the information with the class. Ask students to say which tenses are used in each clause. Give some examples of your own before students work in pairs to complete the sentences.

> **Possible answers**
>
> 1 I'll go with them.
> 2 I'll watch some DVDs
> 3 I won't tidy my room
> 4 I'll buy a computer game
> 5 I'll get up early in the morning.
> 6 I want to buy something in town on Saturday

2 Read through the information with the class. Ask students to say which tenses are used in each clause. Students work in pairs to complete the sentences.

Refer students to the Grammar reference, SB page 85.

Possible answers

1 was / were
2 wouldn't
3 saw / found / discovered / heard
4 would
5 had / won
6 saw

3 Ask students to say when we use *will (not)/would (not)* – not with the *if* clause.

Answers

2 lost
3 won't go
4 woke
5 wouldn't be
6 will drive
7 wouldn't watch
8 will help/'ll help

4 Ask students to complete the exercise individually before comparing their answers. Ask them to look carefully at any answers where they disagree. If they have completed everything correctly, they can either check their answers with another pair, or make some sentences of their own, using both conditionals. These can then be put on the board and checked by the whole class.

Answers

1 I will be very happy if you **come** to my house. / I **would** be very happy if you came to my house.
2 I think your family would be sad and worried if you **didn't** go. / I think your family **will** be sad and worried if you don't go.
3 If I were you, I **would** go to the large school in the centre of town.
4 It would be better if you **went** to his house. / It **will** be better if you go to his house.
5 If you **help** me, it will be better.
6 If you come, **I'll** bring something to drink. / If you **came**, I'd bring something to drink.

5 After working through these points in pairs, students can make their own questions in pairs, writing them on a piece of paper. Give students examples of beginnings for their questions, i.e. *What will you do if ...* , *What would you do if ...* . Discuss some examples and put them on the board before students begin to write their own. Then they walk around the room asking different students their question, and swap papers each time so that they don't always ask the same question.

To round off, you could do a class survey, asking them which item around their home (apart from a computer and a mobile) they would miss if they didn't have it, and why. Ask them if they think their parents would have the same opinion.

See the Workbook and CD ROM for further practice.

Travel & holidays
Reading
Part 5

Exam task

Ask students to look at the photo and think about what's happening – they may already know something about the topic from the news. Ask them to share any information they have with the rest of the class.

Get students to take time to read through the text to see how much they can already understand without the words in the gaps.

Answers

1 C 2 D 3 B 4 A 5 A 6 D 7 C 8 A 9 B 10 D

1 When they've finished the task, ask them to briefly summarise in pairs what they've read about, in their own words.

Then ask them to discuss the points. Ask them the following questions to help them: *What might be exciting about the trip? Why might you feel nervous? What might you see from the windows? The ground? Clouds? A view of earth from a long way up? Stars and planets? How would the view be different from the view out of an aeroplane window?*

CLIL Encourage students to follow the developments of Virgin Galactic's Spaceship Two on the Internet. They could make a timeline to chart its progress.

Listening
Part 4

1 In pairs, get students to answer the questions and talk about what they can see in each picture. Ask them to also think about these two questions: *What would you be able to do in each place? What might be a disadvantage of going there?*

Further practice
When students have finished discussing the photos, ask them to talk about their own holidays and describe them to their partner. *Where do you go? What do you do? Have you been to any of the places in the photos?*

They should make notes before they begin and use these to follow up with a piece of written work.

Discuss as a class.

2 **37** Get students to listen carefully and tick the appropriate boxes. Point out that the items aren't in the same order as the recording, so they have to listen carefully.

Answers

	Jake		Marta	
	☺	☹	☺	☹
the coast	✓			✓
the mountains	✓		✓	
the city centre		✓		✓
an adventure park		✓	✓	
a sports camp	✓		✓	

3 When they've completed the task, ask students to give reasons for their answers, pointing out what each person said.

Exam task

38 Read through the Exam tip and the instructions with the class first. Then get students to read quickly through the questions before they listen.

If students are still struggling with their listening skills, ask them what they can remember about some of the following before they try answering the exam questions, e.g:

- where Joanna and Mark went
- what they wore
- how long they stayed
- Mark's horse
- their meals
- Joanna's first horse
- who was there with them
- Mark's photos

> **Answers**
>
> 1 A They both thought their parents would say no.
> 2 A They had big meals, their own rooms and a pool.
> 3 B '..(teenagers) who hadn't been riding much before..' '… like us!'
> 4 B He didn't really think he might get hurt.
> 5 A He went far too fast and scared her a bit.
> 6 B He's not sure they're brilliant so he might change his mind about displaying them.

Speaking

Part 4

1 Get students to talk about what's happening in the two pictures, and why they would / wouldn't enjoy taking part in the two sports. Remind the students to take turns speaking. Monitor and note down any problems to revise when they have finished the activity. Encourage them to describe as much as they can in the photos, e.g. the weather, background, what people are wearing.

2 **39** Ask students to read through the sentences. Play the recording twice so students can complete them. Check answers as a class.

> **Answers**
>
> 1 I prefer going abroad to staying at home.
> 2 I like going somewhere in my country more than going somewhere far away
> 3 I don't really enjoy it as much as my parents do
> 4 going on holiday is much better than staying at home

Boy: So, tell me about your holidays, Tina. Where do you normally go?

Girl: Well, to be honest I prefer going abroad to staying at home, because we always go somewhere hot – a beach, usually. How about you?

Boy: Well, I like going somewhere in my country more than going somewhere far away. That's really tiring! So we go to our summer house by a lake.

Girl: Do you? That sounds very peaceful – but I'd rather be somewhere lively than somewhere quiet, because I like going shopping and watching live music. You can't do that out in the countryside.

Boy: No, well, I don't really enjoy it as much as my parents do, because I miss my friends. But I read a lot and we do some watersports together, like sailing.

Girl: That's good. Anyway, going on holiday is much better than staying at home, isn't it? That's really boring!

Boy: I agree!

3 (39) Play the recording again. Students compare their answers in pairs. Then check answers as a class.

Answer

Tina prefers going abroad because it is hot.
Greg doesn't like going far away because it's tiring.
Tina prefers lively places because she likes shopping and watching live music.
Greg misses his friends on holiday but he does watersports.
Tina and Greg agree staying at home is boring.

Exam task

Go through the information provided. Ask a few students if they have ever been to any of the locations. Ask others to say what activities they do on holiday, apart from the ones mentioned.

Encourage students to use the ways of expressing preferences that they've just heard in the dialogue above. You could tell pairs of students that you are going to give them a set amount of time (3 minutes) and that they have to try to keep talking during that time. You could put the students into groups of four, so that while one pair is talking, the other group is listening for examples of good language. This will help them prepare for being observed in the exam.

Writing

Part 2

1 Ask students *What kind of photos do you take on holiday - friends and family? views? wildlife? Do you use a camera or your mobile? What do you do with your photos when you get home?* Encourage students to say as much as they possibly can about the photo, using the prompts.

2 Remind students that this is the kind of check they should do on their own writing in the exam. It's particularly important to ensure that errors aren't making the intended meaning unclear.

Answer

Hi Sarah,
You'll never guess what happened during my holiday! I was walking along a road in Croatia where there was a lots of water. Suddenly I saw a boy waterskiing along the **road. It** was amazing! Come to my house tommorrow so that I can to tell **you** about my trip – and show you my **ph**oto!

See you soon.

3 Can students work out what the three points were from the text? It doesn't matter if their answers are not exactly the same as in the book, as long as they are possible.

Answer

1 tell Sarah what you were doing when you took the photo / where you were
2 explain what you saw / who you saw / what the person was doing
3 invite Sarah to come and visit you / arrange a time to show Sarah your photo

4 As an introduction to this exercise, put some examples on the board, e.g. ask students to say what they were doing when you walked into the classroom (*I was talking to my friend. I was sitting quietly. I was eating a sandwich! I was looking at my English book.*)

Answers

I was walking along the road when I saw a man.
My phone rang while I was cycling to football practice.
1 past continuous   2 past simple

5 Students complete the sentences individually. Check answers as a class.

Answers

1 saw   2 was walking   3 ate   4 was sitting   5 arrived
6 were all talking; walked   7 were you doing   8 was buying

See the Workbook for more practice.

6 Put suggested endings to the sentences on the board. Ask them to follow the pattern i.e. *I heard/saw someone doing something.* Which ones do students like the best?

7 You could ask students to prepare in advance for this activity and bring in some unusual photos or pictures of places that they've visited. You could also use photos from magazines and ask them to role play talking about taking the photos on holiday.

Exam task

Read through the instructions and the Exam tip with the class. You could ask the students to write the email in class time under exam conditions.

Sample answer

Hi Marcus,

I'm sending you a photo of me and my family on holiday in Spain. I really like it as my whole family looks happy. Can you send me some of your holiday photos? I'd love to see them!

Best wishes,

Revision key

Unit 1

1 1 is sitting 2 gets up 3 We come; we're living; is working
  4 says; cooks 5 really wants 6 is studying; she's working
  7 I'm not enjoying 8 Do you like

2 1 about 2 in 3 to 4 of 5 at 6 of

3 1 or 2 so 3 because 4 Although 5 and
  6 because 7 but 8 so

4 1 recipe 2 drama 3 watersports 4 volleyball
  5 canteen 6 uniform 7 gym 8 facilities

Unit 2

1 1 didn't arrive/did not arrive 2 were 3 won 4 did Suzy find
  5 became 6 paid 7 felt 8 didn't have/did not have

2 1 were you talking 2 was always having 3 did you have
  4 didn't start 5 Was your dad going 6 was running
  7 did Emily say 8 saw

3 1 gives 2 hand 3 believe 4 join 5 stay 6 give
  7 get 8 stay

4 1 A 2 B 3 C 4 A 5 B 6 B 7 A 8 A

Unit 3

1 1 more interesting 2 as big 3 the best 4 more difficult
  5 worse than 6 more expensive 7 the cheapest
  8 the most comfortable

2 1 where 2 who 3 which 4 where 5 which 6 which
  7 where 8 who

3 1 department store 2 fashionable 3 changing room
  4 size 5 designs 6 refund 7 cash desk 8 reduced

4 1 leather 2 Trainers 3 plain 4 gloves 5 suit
  6 bracelet 7 sandals 8 silver; gold

Unit 4

1 1 I've never been 2 Did Victor go 3 have you known
  4 did you meet 5 We've had 6 they've ever eaten
  7 My brother's always wanted 8 did your teacher find

2 1 B 2 B 3 B 4 C 5 A 6 C 7 A 8 B

3 1 exciting 2 disappointment 3 enjoyable 4 relaxed
  5 organised 6 worry 7 entertaining 8 challenges

4 1 of 2 of 3 about 4 about 5 with 6 by/at 7 about
  8 by

Unit 5

1 1 Could 2 can't 3 mustn't 4 should 5 might 6 could
  7 will 8 might

2 1 A 2 C 3 B 4 B

3 1 cod 2 cabbage 3 Peaches 4 lettuce 5 turkey
  6 Strawberry 7 Beef 8 Tuna

4 1 frozen 2 raw 3 fried 4 boiled

5 1 back 2 on 3 for 4 up

Unit 6

1 1 didn't use to 2 Did you use to 3 didn't use to
  4 used to 5 Did you use to 6 used to

2 1 Karl / him to take 2 forgetting 3 to help 4 living
  5 to take him / Harry 6 travelling 7 going
  8 to buy him / Richard

3 1 made 2 made 3 have 4 go 5 do 6 had

4 1 freezing 2 windy 3 rainy 4 warm 5 snowy

5 1 lively 2 sociable 3 peaceful 4 elderly 5 convenient
  6 huge 7 on the coast 8 an apartment

Unit 7

1 1 had never escaped 2 had been 3 were 4 had travelled
  5 hadn't done 6 weren't 7 didn't find 8 had already made

2 1 have/'ve never seen
  2 will/'ll / are going to do/'re going to do 3 Have you got
  4 am/'m going (to go) 5 did you buy 6 don't use

3 1 whale 2 snake 3 penguin 4 camel 5 spider 6 parrot
  7 bat 8 elephant

4 1 pass on 2 provides 3 carry on 4 escaped
  5 protect 6 solve

Unit 8

1 1 won't 2 Unless 3 sees 4 might 5 won't
  6 if 7 is 8 won't

2 1 didn't want 2 were 3 wouldn't 4 would 5 won
  6 wouldn't 7 asked 8 didn't stay

3 1 wasn't / weren't 2 didn't keep 3 unless 4 wouldn't
  5 would meet 6 don't go

4 1 traffic lights 2 journey 3 platform 4 pilot 5 crowded
  6 motorway 7 check in 8 luggage 9 waves 10 map

Practice test key & recording script

Reading Part 1

1 C   2 B   3 A   4 A   5 C

Reading Part 2

6 C   7 H   8 D   9 F   10 B

Reading Part 3

11 B   12 A   13 A   14 B   15 B   16 A
17 B   18 A   19 B   20 A

Reading Part 4

21 A   22 B   23 B   24 A   25 A

Reading Part 5

26 B   27 B   28 C   29 D   30 A
31 C   32 D   33 B   34 A   35 C

Writing Part 1

1   Anna's friends were
2   invite as/so many
3   for them
4   go home / leave until
5   Did you enjoy

Writing Part 2

6   Hi Sam,
    I've just won an essay competition! I saw it in my favourite
    magazine. My essay was all about the environment, and I got a
    camera as a prize. It's really cool!
    See you soon.
    Best wishes,

Writing Part 3

7   Hi Denise,
    Thanks for your letter. It sounds a good project. Why don't
    you go out and take some photos of the new buildings in your
    city? You should find the really tall ones. Then you could go
    and find some old buildings. You could draw them. You could
    include pictures of your favourite shops and cafés too. And
    don't forget the people – if I were you, I'd get pictures of them
    too. If you put them all in a book, it will be really interesting.
    I hope that helps! Good luck with your project!
    Best wishes

8   I got home from school at 4 o'clock yesterday as usual. When
    I opened the front door, I heard voices. Who was at home?
    Carefully I opened the door of the living room. Mum and dad
    were there – talking to Uncle Jim! He'd just come home from
    Australia after seven years. He brought me lots of presents – a
    book about Australia, a DVD and a toy kangaroo! They were
    cool. Then we had some cake and some drinks. Uncle Jim is
    going back to Australia soon, and I'm going to visit him. I
    can't wait!

Listening Part 1

1 C   2 B   3 B   4 C   5 A   6 C   7 A

Listening Part 2

8 C   9 C   10 B   11 A   12 B   13 B

Listening Part 3

14 pool   15 the USA / America   16 cousin   17 ship
18 dolphins   19 eleven / 11

Listening Part 4

20 B   21 B   22 A   23 A   24 B   25 A

Recording script

Part 1   🔘 40

*There are seven questions in this part. For each question there
are three pictures and a short recording. For each question,
choose the correct answer A, B or C.*
Before we start, here is an example.

What do the students agree needs replacing in their school?

Girl: The head teacher's asked us for ideas on what we
        think need replacing in the school.
Boy: What about an interactive whiteboard for every
        classroom?
Girl: Yeah there aren't enough. And everyone loves them,
        especially the teachers.
Boy: And that would be better than new computers
        because everyone has their own laptop.
Girl: True. And you can use them for everything – you don't
        need to replace textbooks all the time if you have one
        of those to look at in the classroom, because you can
        get digital books.
Boy: Exactly ... well that was an easy decision.

The answer is A.
Look at the three pictures for question 1 now.
*Now we are ready to start. Listen carefully. You will hear each
recording twice.*

1   *What must the boy do after school?*
    Mum: Matthew, remember your piano teacher's cancelled
              your lesson today. It'll be on Thursday instead.
    Matthew: That's good because I need to finish my history
              project this evening, Mum.
    Mum: OK, well do some piano practice if you have time.
              You didn't do much at the weekend.
    Matthew: That's because I spent so much time tidying my
              room! Anyway, I won't have time later. I'll do some
              tomorrow, I promise.
    Mum: OK. I'll remind you then.

2 *What time did the girl's new swimming lesson finish?*

Dad: You're late Michaela. I was getting worried. I thought you'd be home half an hour ago.

Michaela: I told you Dad. I'm in a new swimming class now which goes on until quarter to six. The other one finished at quarter past five so I could get the earlier bus. Now I have to rush out of the pool to make sure I leave the sports centre in time to get the one at quarter past six.

3 *Which animal was the film about?*

Girl: I really enjoyed it. It was much better than the one about sharks. I learned a lot too. I didn't know there weren't any polar bears in that part of the world. And I didn't realise it was the male penguins that sat on the eggs for months in icy winds while the females went off to find food. They're really funny to watch as well – they're so slow on land and so fast in the water. But it's hard to imagine any creature being able to live in such an environment.

4 *What is the boy going to buy at the market?*

Boy: Can I get some strawberries at the market, Mum?

Woman: Well, there are still some in the fridge so we'll get some more next time. I need a coconut because I'm going to make a curry with that and some mango this evening.

Boy: I think we've run out of apples.

Woman: You're right. Get a couple of kilos of those. A pineapple would be nice but I think you'll have enough to carry, so don't worry about that. And I'll get some grapes from the supermarket tomorrow.

Boy: OK.

5 *What will the weather be like on Saturday?*

Man: So moving on to Saturday's forecast ... By Saturday the wind will drop and the weather should be calmer. It should remain dry and bright throughout most of the day with the chance of a few showers. Although the rain won't last long, it could be heavy at times, so definitely worth remembering to take an umbrella with you. The temperature will be average for the time of year ...

6 *What happened to the boy at the basketball match?*

Mum: Tell me about the basketball match, Jon.

Boy: Well, our team played well – we scored loads of points. Then I fell and hurt my leg, but I carried on playing. The other team was really better than us, though.

Mum: So did you lose?

Boy: No, because in the final seconds, I managed to get the ball, jump up to the basket and score! That meant we'd won! I thought my team might carry me out of the gym like a hero, though, so I was a bit disappointed.

Mum: Well, maybe next time ...

7 *What does the girl still want to buy for the party?*

Girl: Hi, Mum! I'm just shopping in town with Hannah, to get some stuff to wear for the party on Saturday. I've found a pair of trousers, but no top to go with them, so we're in Masons department store now. I'm sure we'll get something here. I couldn't find any shoes, either, so I think I'll just wear my old ones. We'll be finished soon – do you want to come and meet us in town? Call me back – bye!

That is the end of Part 1.

Part 2 🔘 41

Now turn to Part 2, questions 8 to 13.
You will hear an interview with an Australian girl called Verity, who has recently been on a student exchange programme. For each question, choose the correct answer A, B or C.
You now have 45 seconds to look at the questions for Part 2.

Now we are ready to start. Listen carefully. You will hear the recording twice.

Interviewer: With me in the studio is Verity Meehan, who's recently returned from a six-month exchange programme with a family in the Netherlands. That's a long way from home, Verity. Why did you choose to do your exchange programme there?

Verity: Well, none of my friends had been there or anything like that but my grandfather spent some time there when he was young and he said I should visit one day and I'd planned to do that as soon as I could. So when I had the opportunity to go to Europe, it seemed like the obvious place to go.

Interviewer: But you were only 15. Was there anything you found difficult about living in a foreign country?

Verity: Well, the family I stayed with in the Netherlands were really kind. And I wasn't lonely because I shared a room with one of their daughters. She helped me get used to my new routine, made sure I got up in time and things like that. The only thing that was hard was the one-kilometre bike ride to school every day! I enjoyed it in the summer but in winter it was terrible.

Interviewer: So, when you arrived, what did you notice straight away about the Netherlands?

Verity: Well, I remember the first few hours really clearly. I knew the weather wouldn't be warm because it was winter, but it wasn't as bad as I'd thought it would be. The family met me at the airport and we drove to their village. I was a bit disappointed by the countryside – it looks much nicer in summer – but I was so excited when I saw all the old buildings there. They looked exactly how I thought they would.

Interviewer: And what was the school like?

Verity: It was OK because there were a lot of classes in English. And they gave me projects to do when there were subjects in Dutch I couldn't understand. The school was very modern and much bigger than most schools in Australia. The library was fantastic and they also had a lot more science labs than my school at home.

Interviewer:	What about the students?
Verity:	Oh, they were really friendly. They gave me lots of advice about places I should visit. They'd all travelled a lot more than me, although no one had been to Australia. But what I found really strange was that they'd never thought about going away from their families for several months like me. Some of them couldn't understand how I could do that.
Interviewer:	So is this an experience you'd recommend?
Verity:	Oh, definitely. I think six months was the right amount of time. I needed that amount of time to learn the language. But after six months I really needed to see my parents. I was so happy to see them again.

That is the end of Part 2.

Now turn to Part 3, questions 14 to 19.

Part 3 42

You will hear a boy called Jake talking to his classmates about a diving trip he recently did with his family.
For each question, fill in the missing information in the numbered space.

You now have 20 seconds to look at Part 3.

Now we are ready to start. Listen carefully. You will hear the recording twice.

My name's Jake, and I recently went on a fantastic diving trip with my family – swimming under the water!

It was very exciting. I'd never gone diving in open water before, like a river or a lake. I'd just done my diving training in a pool. But I was really looking forward to my first real sea dive, so off we went. We couldn't decide where to go at first. We considered going somewhere in Europe, but then friends in the USA offered to let us stay with them, so we went to the coast there, where there were perfect diving conditions.

On the first day we went out in a boat with our instructor and other people learning to dive. My father stayed in the boat, and my cousin jumped into the sea at the same time as me. I was excited, although a bit scared too, as the water was deep. As we swam down, we saw lots of strange sights – a huge plant growing underwater, some shells, and my favourite thing of all, a ship! It had been there many years, and it was fascinating to look at.

I was a bit worried as we were swimming around because we'd heard there might be sharks in the area – only small ones, but it didn't matter! So I was very scared when some big creatures came swimming towards us – but they turned out to be dolphins! They played with us in the water. We even managed to get some photos. We hoped we'd see some flying fish – but no such luck!

Each day's dives were completely different. We did three dives on the first day, and four on the second, plus a few more – eleven dives altogether, including a night dive! I even got a diving qualification at the end of it all! It was the best trip ever.

That is the end of Part 3.

Now turn to Part 4, questions 20 to 25.

Part 4 43

Look at the six sentences for this part.
You will hear a conversation between a boy, Harry, and a girl, Laura, about wildlife photography.
Decide if each sentence is correct or incorrect.
If it is correct, put a tick (✓) in the box under A for YES. If it is not correct, put a tick (✓) in the box under B for NO.

You now have 20 seconds to look at the questions for Part 4.

Now we are ready to start. Listen carefully. You will hear the recording twice.

Harry:	Hi, Laura. Have you seen these wildlife photos in *Animals* magazine? They're the winners of the recent competition.
Laura:	Let's see, Harry. Mm, there are some good ones – that fish is great. You can see it quite clearly under the water.
Harry:	Mm, the sun's shining brightly on the water, though – it'd be better without that. The one of the tiger's brilliant, I think.
Laura:	But I prefer photos of the things you might find living in your garden. Tigers always look wonderful so anyone can take a brilliant shot of them – just go to the local zoo ...
Harry:	Well, you've got a point. That's why I like your photos – all your pictures of frogs and stuff – they're common animals, but you make them look special.
Laura:	Thanks, Harry! I think it's more about being lucky, though – and not moving! And it isn't easy when you're watching wild creatures and not making any movement but they'll run away if you do.
Harry:	I know what you mean. I've missed some great photos by moving at the last minute. Anyway, the other thing's my camera.
Laura:	What about it?
Harry:	Well, it's not like yours. Maybe I need a more advanced one to get the photos I want.
Laura:	It's fine – you just need to learn more about how to use it. I bet it's got buttons you haven't even tried yet!
Harry:	Hmm, maybe – I'm often disappointed with my pictures, though. I'm thinking of going out before five in the morning and going down to the park.
Laura:	Well, there won't be many people around then. You could get the same pictures later in the day, though, just by being a bit more creative in how you look at things. Anyway, what about the photography course at the college in town – have you decided yet? We'd learn a lot.
Harry:	Well, I do need to know more about techniques – but I can always just ask my brother if I've got a question. But I _am_ thinking about it ...
Laura:	Well, it's up to you ...

Workbook key & recording script

Unit 1

Grammar

1 1 is 2 come 3 are living 4 is working 5 are staying
6 find 7 love 8 is 9 doesn't rain 10 feel 11 are
12 don't get

2 1 to, e 2 about, b 3 of, a 4 of, f 5 to, c 6 at, d

3 1 Sam can't stand washing up/ doing the washing-up / washing the dishes.

2 Debbie quite likes cooking / making food / preparing food.

3 Jon doesn't mind walking the dog / taking the dog for a walk.

4 Sara hates travelling by bus / getting the bus / going on the bus.

5 Karl enjoys playing computer games / using his computer.

Vocabulary

1 1 generous 2 funny 3 sociable 4 lazy 5 honest
6 patient 7 easy going 8 cheerful

2 1 performs 2 get 3 wear 4 canteen 5 pitch 6 lab
7 hand in 8 going on

3 1 suggested 2 apologising 3 describes 4 invited
5 explaining 6 advised 7 persuade 8 thank 9 warns

Exam tasks

Writing Part 2

1 1 so 2 or 3 because 4 Although 5 but 6 and then

2 Sample answer

Hi, Jan

I've just taken up tennis! But I haven't got a racket or any tennis shoes, so I need to go and buy some. Would you like to come into town with me? You could help me choose. Hope to see you soon.

(44 words)

Reading Part 2

1 F 2 B 3 D 4 H 5 E

Listening Part 4 🔘 02

1 B 2 A 3 A 4 A 5 B 6 A

Recording script	
Girl:	How's the decorating going in your room, Mark? Is it finished yet?
Boy:	It's going OK. Come in and have a look at the changes.
Girl:	Oh, it looks completely different! You've taken out the spare bed and moved the wardrobe. Still, I guess your mum was happy with that. She never really liked the furniture in here, did she?
Boy:	Well, it was quite old, so she thought it was time I had new stuff. We painted the walls, too.
Girl:	Yeah – I didn't know you'd chosen purple. That's your favourite though, isn't it?
Boy:	Mmm, it's made it darker in here, but I don't mind that – it means I can see my computer screen better!
Girl:	Well, I'm looking forward to changing my room too. The thing is, whatever I do with it, I'm never going to find enough space for all my things.
Boy:	Well, that's because you've got so many clothes! I know what you mean though. My room's pretty full, too. I've stored lots of things under my bed, but that hasn't improved it much.
Girl:	But you got rid of lots of your old magazines and computer games. Still, you were never going to look at them again, were you?
Boy:	I guess not. I'm kind of sorry I did that now, though. My mate at school's got them all – I might ask him if I can borrow them sometimes.
Girl:	Oh Mark! Well, my mum's offered to buy me a new wardrobe and drawers for my room, so that I have somewhere to put things, but to be honest I prefer what I've got now. I've grown up with it, really.
Boy:	Yeah. Anyway, we're lucky to have our own rooms, aren't we? A lot of my school friends share with older brothers or sisters – that must be annoying.
Girl:	Mmm, but then I guess you get to use their things and you don't have to buy your own!
Boy:	True – even my brother's not bad at sharing his things with me!

Reading Part 5

1 B 2 C 3 B 4 D 5 A 6 B 7 C 8 C 9 B 10 C

Unit 2

Grammar

1 1 became 2 began 3 brought 4 bought 5 caught
6 chose 7 drank 8 fell 9 felt 10 grew 11 left 12 lost
13 rang 14 ran 15 spoke 16 took 17 threw 18 woke
19 wore 20 wrote

2 2 Maya ran 10 km every day.

3 Maya felt nervous.

4 Maya went to bed early.

5 Maya didn't work hard.

6 Maya didn't get up early.

7 Maya ate lots of chocolate.

3 2 was travelling 3 wasn't feeling 4 was getting
5 were feeling 6 were clapping and shouting
7 were celebrating

Vocabulary

1 stay 2 burst 3 defeated 4 talent 5 disappointment
6 attitude 7 lost 8 achieve

Exam tasks

Listening Part 3

1 check   **2** 24   **3** Myerson   **4** blue   **5** ten   **6** 30th September

> **Recording script**
>
> OK everyone. As it's the start of the season I want to remind you all about our team rules. So, first of all, no friends or family members are allowed in the changing room. Also a new rule – each week a different pair of students will have to check that no one has left anything behind after every game or practice session. That way I hope you won't lose as much of your stuff as last season.
>
> Next, some rules about matches. Obviously it's a big problem for the team if someone is missing so please contact me as soon as possible if there's a problem. Half an hour before the match isn't good enough. Even two or three hours doesn't really give me enough time – I need at least 24 hours' notice. Of course, I know sometimes there will be last-minute emergencies. If I'm not available, then please call our new assistant coach, Jim Myerson. That's M-Y-E-R-S-O-N on 099879654.
>
> Now, I hope you like the new red team shirts I think they're pretty cool. And I don't want anyone to spoil the effect by wearing black or white shorts and socks – remember only blue is acceptable.
>
> OK. I think that's almost everything. Just a word about arrangements for games away from home. It's really important that we arrive 30 minutes before the match starts so we can warm up. Which means the bus must leave on time. So can I ask you all to aim to arrive at least ten minutes before departure time? Thank you.
>
> It's also essential that you don't forget the dates and times of each match as well. So the first one is on the 30th of September, not August, as it says on the original calendar. Good. Any questions?

Reading Part 5

1 A   **2** B   **3** B   **4** C   **5** D   **6** A   **7** D   **8** C   **9** C   **10** D

Writing Part 3

2   **1** b   **2** a   **3** d   **4** e   **5** c

Unit 3

Grammar

1   **1** much more   **2** as   **3** the most   **4** the prettiest   **5** the best
6 worse

2   **1** more expensive than   **2** cheaper than   **3** as good as
4 the furthest   **5** as heavy as   **6** the most crowded
7 the worst   **8** bigger than

3   **1** where we had some delicious chocolate cake

2 which was very disappointing

3 where we saw some ancient jewellery

4 who explained the maths homework for me again

5 who agreed to lend me her favourite dress for the party

6 which he was really excited about

4   **1** pretty pale pink

2 valuable old silver

3 big black leather

4 dark red cotton

5 blue, black and green

6 two old gold

Vocabulary

1   **1** put, on   **2** wears   **3** try, on   **4** took, off   **5** get dressed
6 dressed   **7** change

2   Suggested answers
1 The girl is wearing a T-shirt, a skirt, a bracelet, sandals, a ring, a belt and a jacket.

2 The boy is wearing a sweatshirt, jeans, trainers, socks, a watch, a scarf and gloves.

Exam tasks

Listening Part 2 04

1 B   **2** A   **3** C   **4** B   **5** C   **6** A

> **Recording script**
>
> **Interviewer:** Hi everyone! Today I'm with 16-year-old Nicky, who has her own fashion blog online – and it's very popular! Welcome, Nicky. What made you want to start your blog?
>
> **Nicky:** Well, I guess it was because of the area where I live – near a small town. Although lots of young people there love fashion, there's hardly anywhere you can buy the latest clothes. We're lucky in some ways because at least our school lets us wear what we like. But I felt we all needed somewhere to find out more about fashion, so that gave me the idea.
>
> **Interviewer:** So why do you think your blog's been so successful?
>
> **Nicky:** Well, I always put information on it about designers and what they've got in their latest fashion shows, and that's usually exactly what all the celebrities are wearing. But I believe lots of people look at the blog because they're just like me – they can't afford top designers' stuff and they know they'll find things there that don't cost a huge amount.
>
> **Interviewer:** Did you have problems setting up the blog?
>
> **Nicky:** Well, luckily my older brother's really into computers, so he gave me good advice. But it was a while before anyone contacted me, so I was worried that no one was interested! That didn't last long, though, especially when I started adding pictures of clothes I'd chosen and put together. They give people ideas about what to wear.
>
> **Interviewer:** And you recently produced an amazing dress for a student fashion show, didn't you?
>
> **Nicky:** Oh, yes! My friends and I all follow a TV series about film stars and what they wear, so for the student fashion show, we decided to produce something that a star might wear for a big occasion. My friends tried to copy dresses from different designers. But I just created one made from my mum's old curtains! And everyone loved it!

Interviewer:	And now because of your blog you get invited to some big fashion shows, don't you? Do you enjoy that?
Nicky:	It's wonderful! I mean, I've only got an old camera at the moment, so I don't get great photos of the models, but it's just such an exciting place to be. And the models look fabulous, although I'd love to know what they really think about the clothes!
Interviewer:	And what do your parents think about your blog?
Nicky:	Well, I was worried they'd say I shouldn't spend so much time on it, in case they thought I should concentrate on schoolwork instead. But they soon realised just how much I loved it, so now they're happy for me.
Interviewer:	Thanks Nicky!

Reading Part 5

1 B 2 D 3 C 4 D 5 B 6 A 7 C 8 C 9 B 10 A

Writing Part 3

Sample answer

Hi Jo,

Thanks for the lovely photo of yourself in your favourite clothes! I like wearing quite casual clothes, too, like jeans and T-shirts, but I also like putting on something smart if I'm going to a party or somewhere special. I have to wear school uniform all week, so I like a change!

I often go to town with my friends to buy clothes, but I like looking at things online too. My mum sometimes orders things for me, which is great because I can try them on at home to see if I like them. Do you ever buy things online?

Hope to hear from you soon,

Best wishes,

Reading Part 1

1 B 2 A 3 C 4 B 5 C

Unit 4

Grammar

1 1 have seen   2 have you been   3 haven't decided
   4 have had   5 hasn't chosen   6 has won

2 1 B 2 C 3 B 4 A 5 A 6 B 7 A

3 1 have known   2 chosen   3 two years ago   4 has
   5 received   6 haven't answered, I've been   7 forgotten

Vocabulary

1 2 e enjoyable   3 h organised   4 g scary   5 b nervous
   6 c worried   7 d anxious   8 a terrific   9 f exciting

2 1 of   2 by   3 about   4 by / about   5 of / about   6 of
   7 about   8 with

3 1 surprise   2 determined   3 interesting   4 bored   5 afraid
   6 keen   7 amazing   8 entertainment

Exam tasks

Reading Part 5

1 B 2 C 3 A 4 D 5 B 6 D 7 C 8 A 9 A 10 C

Listening Part 1

1 A 2 B 3 C 4 C 5 B 6 B 7 A

Recording script

1	*What does the girl still need to do?*
Kendra:	I'm going to the cinema with Sophie later, OK, Mum?
Mum:	Yes, but make sure you've done everything before you go. Have you phoned Grandma yet?
Kendra:	Yes, but she was out.
Mum:	Well ring her again before you leave.
Kendra:	OK. Well that's all I have to do because I've already walked the dog and I went to get the eggs and milk from the shop this morning.
Mum:	Oh, that's fine then.
2	*On which day does the man decide to get his son tickets for the concert?*
Man:	My son's just tried to book some tickets for the Black Keys concert on March 21st but there's a problem with your website.
Woman:	I'm sorry about that. There are only the most expensive tickets left for that date, I'm afraid.
Man:	What about the 20th? Have you got any for £25?
Woman:	Sorry, those are all sold out – but there are some on the 19th. Or there are 35 pound ones available on the 20th.
Man:	Yes, those would be best. The 19th is no good because he's got school the next day.
Woman:	OK. How many ...
3	*Which instrument is it possible to start learning?*
Teacher:	OK everyone, I've got an announcement to make about music lessons. I'm afraid it won't be possible for anyone new to join any of the guitar groups as they're all full. But if anyone is interested in taking up the violin there are now some places available in the beginners' class. So let me know as soon as possible if you're interested. Unfortunately we won't be able to offer drum lessons for the moment because we haven't been able to find a new drums teacher.
4	*What do the boys decide to do on Saturday?*
Alex:	What shall we do on Saturday, Harry?
Harry:	We could go to the cinema. Dexter is on.
Alex:	I've already seen it.
Harry:	Well let's do something. I'm bored of staying in and playing computer games all the time.
Alex:	Me too. Well what about going to see Jude's brother's band? They're playing at the sports club. I've never seen them, so I don't know if they're any good.
Harry:	Sounds like it's worth trying. And better than doing nothing.
Alex:	I think so too.

Writing Part 1

1 has been 2 as big as 3 (very) excited
4 haven't / have not sold 5 enjoyable

Unit 5

Grammar

1 1 am playing / 'm playing 2 will win 3 is going to take
  4 will come 5 is opening

2 1 are, must 2 is, mustn't 3 aren't, can't
  4 isn't, don't have to 5 is, can't

3 1 must 2 mustn't 3 may 4 should 5 don't have to
  6 might

Vocabulary

1 2 healthiest 3 fitness 4 Cooking 5 unhealthy 6 unfit
  7 boiled 8 fried

2 1 away 2 back 3 up 4 for 5 on 6 down

3 1 A 2 C 3 B 4 C 5 A 6 C

Exam tasks

Listening Part 3 06

1 1,000 2 ship 3 eggs 4 shower 5 rubbish 6 icezone

> **Recording script**
>
> Hi. My name's Daniela Jefferies and I'm a research scientist
> at the largest station in Antarctica. A station is basically where
> all the scientists live and work. Most people only spend a few
> months of the year working there, usually over the summer,
> when there can be as many as 1,000 people at our station,
> with a total population in Antarctica of around 8,000 people.
> This number drops during the winter when conditions are much
> harder. It's dark all the time and most people stay inside the
> station 24 hours a day. It's possible to fly there by helicopter or
> sea plane but most people travel to the station by ship.
>
> As you can imagine, life in Antarctica is very different to
> life at home. The food is actually really good and meals are
> very sociable as we all eat together in the canteen. There's
> quite a lot of fish on the menu, but things like eggs and fresh
> vegetables soon run out. We have to be careful about the
> amount of water we use as all the water has to be made from
> sea water. This means that when the station is crowded, you
> often can't have a daily shower.
>
> Another thing we have to be very careful about is recycling. As
> much as possible is recycled because any rubbish produced
> on the station that can't be recycled has to be taken away from
> the Antarctic twice a year to help protect the environment.
> But generally life is comfortable enough and you have such
> amazing opportunities to be in one of the wildest and most
> beautiful landscapes in the world.
>
> If you're interested in finding out more, you can follow my blog
> – the address is www. icezone.org. That's I-C-E-Z-O-N-E – all
> one word, dot org. Now I'd be very happy to answer any of
> your questions ....

Reading Part 5

1 B 2 C 3 C 4 B 5 D 6 C 7 D 8 B 9 A 10 D

Writing Part 2

1 Would you like to come with us? / It would be great if you
  could come too.

2 I've heard it's really good. / It's one of my favourite films.

3 Why don't we meet at 6.30? / What/How about meeting at
  6.30?

Sample answer

Hi Jon

I'm going to the cinema with my friends tonight. Would you like
to come? We are going to see The Incredibles because I love
adventure films. The movie starts at 7 so how about meeting at
6.30. We are going to wait for you in the food area.

Andy

Unit 6

Grammar

1 1 Did you use to 2 didn't use to 3 didn't use to 4 used to
  5 used to 6 did you use to 7 didn't use to 8 used to

2
infinitive	-ing form
choose	avoid
manage	look forward to
intend	suggest
remind	apologise for
offer	imagine
persuade	miss

3 1 living 2 to help 3 going 4 to have 5 to take 6 seeing

4 1 make / have 2 went 3 didn't do
  4 couldn't / didn't make 5 make 6 go

Vocabulary

1 1 tower 2 palace 3 library 4 museum 5 gallery
  6 city 7 village 8 forest

2 1 lively 2 cosy 3 elderly 4 convenient 5 historical
  6 traditional 7 cultural 8 sociable

Exam tasks

Reading Part 5

1 D 2 C 3 A 4 C 5 A 6 B 7 C 8 B 9 A 10 D

Reading Part 4

1 C 2 A 3 B 4 B 5 C

Listening Part 1 07

1 B 2 B 3 C 4 B 5 A 6 C 7 C

Recording script

1   *Where is the girl's father working now?*

Boy: Your father's a chemist in a big company, isn't he, Andrea? That must be interesting. But does he have to spend much time in an office?

Girl: Oh, he was doing that last year, but he didn't enjoy it very much. So they offered him a place back in one of their laboratories, which he likes much better. He's very interested in doing experiments.

Boy: And does he still want to do some teaching?

Girl: He'll do some later in the year, but he's too busy at the moment.

2   *Which part of the castle did the girl like?*

Boy: How was your visit to the castle, Jackie?

Girl: Well, I had no idea parts of it were so high! We climbed right up to the top of a tower and looked down. But it was really scary – and freezing, too, so I had to come down again. And that's when I saw the huge windows, all made of coloured glass. I'd never seen anything like that before – I bought loads of postcards!

Boy: When we went, we spent ages walking around outside in the gardens.

Girl: Oh, we missed that – it was just so cold!

3   *Where does James live?*

Girl: Hi, James! I haven't seen you for ages! I went past your house last week – I was going to knock on your door and say hello!

Boy: Well, it's lucky you didn't – my parents bought a new flat in town, so we're there now!

Girl: Really? In one of those big new apartment blocks in the centre?

Boy: Oh, they're really expensive, so my parents chose a smaller place, just above a café. It's lovely inside. So come and see us!

Girl: Thanks. I will!

4   *Where will Denise wait for her friend?*

Girl: Hi, Magda. It's Denise. I hope you still want to meet in town. I'm at the tennis courts – my class was over a bit early, so I'm walking towards the big old clock in the centre of town – you know the one? Let's meet there, and then we can decide what to do. I've still got my birthday money to spend, so I'd really like to have a look in the new department store. What do you think? Ring me when you get this. See you soon!

5   *Which of his photos is the boy most satisfied with?*

Boy: I got a new camera for my birthday last year, and I've taken loads of pictures with it. We went on holiday to Egypt just afterwards, so I got lots of photos of the pyramids, but I wasn't used to handling my camera then, so the light wasn't quite right – not like in the ones of the windmill. That's just down the road from where we live. Anyway, I'm off on a school trip to visit the old palace in the capital soon. That should produce some great pictures!

6   *What isn't working in Sarah's room?*

Boy: I don't know how you can sit and do your homework in here, Sarah – it's so cold! Why haven't you switched your heater on?

Girl: Oh, dad fixed it yesterday so it should be OK now. It'll soon warm up the room. Anyway, I didn't notice – I was too busy working on my laptop.

Boy: Well, I've come to borrow your lamp – I still haven't got one and my room's really dark.

Girl: Well, that one won't help you – I knocked it over, so it needs a new light bulb.

Boy: Oh, great!

7   *What was the weather like in their area yesterday?*

Boy: Did you go out with your family yesterday, Marcia?

Girl: We'd planned to go to the beach, but then the weather forecast said it was going to rain, so we didn't organise anything. But that forecast was actually wrong, wasn't it?

Boy: Yeah. I went to the beach for a while. It was great to be outside in warm sunshine – it can be quite windy there sometimes. There weren't many people around, though.

Girl: No – well, they'd probably all heard the same forecast as my family!

Unit 7

Grammar

1   **1** saw, hadn't realised   **2** decided, had never escaped
    3 was, had lived   **4** didn't become, had found
    5 hadn't been, arrived   **6** got, had been

2   **1** haven't seen   **2** don't leave   **3** you ever been
    4 promise we'll/will go   **5** 're/are getting   **6** you like to
    7 want you to   **8** Do you want

Vocabulary

1   **1** conservation   **2** cages   **3** environment   **4** rare
    5 forbidden   **6** wildlife

2   **1** d   **2** c   **3** e   **4** a   **5** f   **6** b

3   **1** B   **2** B   **3** A   **4** B   **5** B   **6** C

Exam tasks

Listening Part 2 08

1 C   **2** A   **3** B   **4** B   **5** B   **6** C

Recording script

Adam: With me here in the studio today is Dr Jenny Borthwick, who's an expert on dolphin behaviour. So how did you first get interested in dolphins?

Jenny: We didn't live near the coast so I'd only seen dolphins in the zoo and it wasn't until I saw a film about them on TV that I fell in love with them.

Adam: So you never went to a dolphin park?

Jenny: No. Never!

Adam: So I suppose you don't like the plan to open a new dolphin park?

Jenny:	No, I don't. Dolphins should be free and in the wild. Some people say that dolphins enjoy performing because they love playing games and doing tricks. But the problem is that in most dolphin parks, dolphins have to work very long hours without a break and this is very cruel.
Adam:	Is there any scientific research to show that these dolphins are unhappy?
Jenny:	Oh yes, lots. We've known for a long time that being in a small pool makes them bored and depressed. Also, they're used to swimming in very deep water and can stay under for 20 minutes. But what we've learned lately is that they dislike the loud clapping and shouting of the crowd watching them perform.
Adam:	That's interesting. But the dolphins don't seem unhappy because they're sociable and like living in groups, don't they?
Jenny:	Yes but the problem with the groups is these aren't the same as in the wild. The main type of dolphin at dolphin parks is bottlenose dolphins. Some of them are separated from their mothers when they're babies and trained to be a performing dolphin, which is obviously very stressful. Other dolphins are caught when they're older and the very strong relationships they have with the other dolphins in their group or pod, as it's called, are broken. These aren't just families. You sometimes get a pod which just consists of young male dolphins for example.
Adam:	What about their food? Is that different to the wild too?
Jenny:	Yes. Instead of spending their time hunting and catching fish, they have to eat dead fish, which isn't the same thing at all. Sometimes they don't get enough to eat – they're given one small meal a day and then get the rest as a reward for performing well.
Adam:	And I imagine you don't think people should swim with dolphins.
Jenny:	It can be a wonderful experience but it can make dolphins act in ways which aren't natural. They become like pets. And this is doing a lot of damage to dolphin relationships.
Adam:	That's very interesting, Jenny. After the break we'll take some questions from listeners ...

Reading Part 5

1 D   **2** C   **3** B   **4** A   **5** A   **6** B   **7** C   **8** D   **9** B   **10** A

Writing Part 1

1 **1** have been   **2** use   **3** had never seen
   4 Nobody has ever asked   **5** better

2 **1** don't be   **2** were more   **3** were given   **4** first time any
   5 we have ever

Unit 8

Grammar

1 **1** rains, 'll put up   **2** 's/is, 'll put on   **3** 's/is, 'll wear
   4 snows, 'll go   **5** 's/is, 'll stay

2 **1** doesn't   **2** unless   **3** might   **4** will   **5** doesn't
   6 won't   **7** if   **8** might

3 **1** had, would / could   **2** wouldn't, were   **3** would, lost
   4 would, was/were, wouldn't   **5** had, would
   6 wouldn't, came

4 **1** unless   **2** didn't   **3** would / could go   **4** I were
   5 helped   **6** 'd/would watch

Vocabulary

1 traffic jam   **2** harbour   **3** waves, rough   **4** speed limit
5 motorway   **6** roundabouts

Exam tasks

Reading Part 3

1 A   **2** A   **3** B   **4** A   **5** B   **6** A   **7** B   **8** A   **9** B   **10** A

Reading Part 5

1 C   **2** D   **3** B   **4** A   **5** C   **6** D   **7** B   **8** B   **9** C   **10** B

Listening Part 4 🔊 09

1 B   **2** B   **3** A   **4** B   **5** A   **6** B

Recording script	
Girl:	Hi, Harry. What's that you're making? It looks like a model spaceship – out of toy building bricks!
Boy:	That's exactly what it is! It's for the school science competition – I'm hoping it's going to travel into space!
Girl:	Wow! It's a bit like the one we saw in the video that our teacher showed us – the one built by a teenager.
Boy:	Yeah, but I'd already got this idea even before I watched the video. I'm trying to build one to my own design.
Girl:	Wow – that's amazing! And it looks almost finished – nearly ready to fly.
Boy:	Well, the model spaceship is done, but I'm working on ideas for how to get it to fly. It's unlikely to be taking off for quite a while – I'm still having problems with the balloon I need to use. And I want it to go up to 35,000 metres.
Girl:	Well, the boy in the video achieved that, and he had similar equipment to you, so I don't see why yours won't be just as good.
Boy:	No, I think it should be OK ...
Girl:	Maybe you should ask someone to give you some help. I mean, I'd love to, but I've got so much homework. I bet our physics teacher, Mr Barnes, would be really interested, though.
Boy:	Yeah, but teachers aren't really allowed to help. Anyway, the other thing I need to do is find somewhere to fly it. My back garden's too small.
Girl:	Well, there's the big park outside town – that isn't usually very busy.
Boy:	Hmm – I could ask my dad to drive me there. That's not a bad idea, Emma. So after all this, you should come and watch the spaceship on its first flight.
Girl:	Mm, I'd like to – when will it be?
Boy:	As soon as it's ready. It'll be early morning, though – say 6.00 a.m.?
Girl:	Right – well, in that case you might have to go without me. I'm not really an early-morning person...
Boy:	Oh, Emma!

Vocabulary extra key

Unit 1

1 **1** flying a kite   **2** building a remote control car
   3 playing the guitar   **4** drawing cartoons
   5 playing volleyball   **6** writing stories   **7** acting on stage
   8 cooking a meal

2 **1** c   **2** e   **3** f   **4** g   **5** h   **6** b   **7** d   **8** a

3 **1** eats   **2** attend   **3** went   **4** passes   **5** made
   6 working / to work   **7** played   **8** arrived

Unit 2

1 **1** h diving board   **2** d hockey stick   **3** g tennis racket
   4 b locker room   **5** c golf course   **6** e football pitch
   7 f running track   **8** a squash court

2 **1** high jump   **2** boxing   **3** skiing   **4** cycling
   5 skateboarding   **6** gymnastics

3 **1** gave up   **2** believe in   **3** hand in   **4** joined in
   5 stays in   **6** get in

Unit 3

1 **1** collar   **2** pocket   **3** sleeve   **4** button

2
J	J	E	A	N	S	H	I	R	T
L	E	A	T	H	E	R	D	S	N
C	W	R	J	A	C	K	E	T	O
Z	E	R	T	T	O	P	Z	P	U
C	L	I	G	H	T	B	L	U	E
K	L	N	O	B	T	O	C	R	G
B	E	G	V	M	O	O	D	P	A
A	R	S	U	I	N	T	Z	L	M
U	Y	S	N	F	E	S	W	E	S

   jeans   top   earrings
   shirt   light blue   hat
   leather   cotton   boots
   jacket   jewellery   purple

3 **1** casual   **2** high   **3** loose   **4** take off   **5** fit   **6** colourful
   7 traditional   **8** natural

Unit 4

1 **Across**
   3 flute   **6** trumpet
   Down
   1 violin   **2** keyboard   **4** drums   **5** guitar

2 **1** excited   **2** worried   **3** relaxing   **4** entertainment
   5 organisation   **6** disappointment   **7** challenge   **8** worry

3 un-: unenjoyable, unsuccessful, unlikely, unsociable,
   unbelievable
   -less: hopeless, careless, useless
   in-: inexpensive, inconvenient

Unit 5

1 **1** pineapple   **2** peach   **3** strawberry   **4** coconut
   5 grapes   **6** pear

2
Meat	Vegetables	Dairy
sausage	broccoli	cheese
lamb	cauliflower	milk
burger	peas	yoghurt

3 **1** E   **2** B   **3** F   **4** A   **5** D   **6** C

Unit 6

1 **1** kettle   **2** central heating   **3** fridge   **4** washing machine
   5 air conditioning   **6** dishwasher   **7** oven   **8** microwave

2 **1** ceiling   **2** tap   **3** basin   **4** rug   **5** pillow   **6** cushion
   7 duvet   **8** dustbin   **9** toilet   **10** balcony   **11** ladder
   12 chest of drawers   **13** wardrobe   **14** cooker
   15 armchair   **16** curtains   **17** mirror   **18** roof   **19** stairs
   20 sink   **21** upstairs   **22** downstairs

3 **1** reception   **2** laboratory   **3** cottage   **4** fire station
   5 studio   **6** stadium

Unit 7

1 **1** kangaroo **2** frog **3** donkey **4** tiger **5** giraffe **6** goat

2

Insect	Baby animal	Bird
bee	kitten	parrot
mosquito	lamb	penguin
fly	puppy	duck

3 **Across**

1 d breeze **4** a peak **6** b sand **7** c stream

Down

2 f rock **3** g leaves **5** e cave

Unit 8

1 **1** d **2** h **3** i **4** c **5** g **6** b **7** j **8** a **9** e **10** f

2 **1** out of **2** by **3** on **4** off **5** on **6** on **7** into **8** on

3 **1** weigh **2** crowded **3** security **4** departure **5** delayed
6 board **7** take off **8** flight **9** landed **10** luggage

Progress test 1 Units 1–2

1 Match answers a–f with 1–6.

1 What's your favourite lesson?
2 What do you like doing in your free time?
3 Do you speak more than two languages?
4 What's your favourite shop?
5 Where do you live?
6 Tell me about your brother.

a Yes, I do. I learn English and French at school, and I speak Spanish.
b Playing my guitar and meeting my friends.
c In Sarcelles, near Paris in France.
d He's very friendly but he's really untidy!
e I really like English but I love Maths.
f A department store in my town. It's got great clothes.

2 Complete the telephone conversation with the correct form of the verbs in brackets. Use the present simple or the present continuous.

Luca: Hi, is that Bruno? It's Luca here.
Bruno: Hi, Luca. What (1) .... (you/do)?
Luca: I (2) .... (watch) the TV but it's not very interesting.
Bruno: (3) .... (you/want) to come round to my house? My brothers and I (4) .... (play) volleyball in the garden.
Luca: Oh, thanks but I can't. I (5) .... (look) after my little sister. My mother always (6) .... (visit) her sister on Saturday afternoon and my father often (7) .... (work). My sister (8) .... (do) her homework at the moment. I usually (9) .... (make) her something to eat after that.
Bruno: What (10) .... (you/usually/cook) her?
Luca: A cheese sandwich!

3 Choose the best answer (a, b or c) to complete each sentence.

1 How do you get to school?
a Yes, I do.
b By bus.
c I go to school.

2 Why didn't you phone me yesterday?
a I'm sorry.
b No, I didn't.
c Phoned you.

3 .... our school is small, it's very good.
a If
b Despite
c Although

4 .... I tidy my room, my mother is very happy!
a Unless
b Although
c If

5 .... losing, Mark is still smiling.
a Despite
b Because
c Although

6 I was thirsty .... I drank a bottle of water.
a so
b because
c but

7 I can't come to the cinema this afternoon .... I'm going to the dentist.
a so
b because
c but

8 My sister always .... good grades in English.
a performs
b passes
c gets

Compact Preliminary for Schools by Sue Elliott and Amanda Thomas © Cambridge University Press 2013 **Photocopiable**

4 Choose the best word to complete the sentences.

1 She *beat / won* the gold medal.
2 The teacher wants us to hand *in / from* our homework tomorrow morning.
3 I can't find my key so I can't *stay / get* in my house.
4 He wins because he *gives / believes* in himself.
5 He's a good goalkeeper. He *defends / defeats* very well.
6 Can your team *succeed / achieve* in winning the World Cup?
7 My team *lost / failed* in the final.
8 He's such a bad loser. He has a really *positive / negative* attitude.

5 Complete the text with the correct form of the verbs in brackets. Use the past simple or the past continuous.

Last Saturday morning I (1) .... (feel) very happy. My team (2) .... (play) in the final of a volleyball tournament and I (3) .... (be) the captain. I (4) .... (have) a large breakfast and then my parents (5) .... (drive) me to the sports centre. Lots of people (6) .... (wait) for the tournament to start. I (7) .... (meet) my team and our coach. We (8) .... (put) on our trainers and shorts when our coach (9) .... (give) us some very good advice. Then it was time to start. (10) .... (we/win)? Of course we did!

6 Complete the sentences with the words in the box.

| fond afraid enjoy interested worried |
| looking forward can't stand good |

1 I .... playing volleyball but I don't want to watch people playing it.
2 I'm .... of climbing trees. I don't like heights.
3 I .... watching cricket. It's so boring.
4 I'm .... about playing my tennis match tomorrow. I don't want to lose.
5 I'm very .... of cooking. I make cakes for my family every weekend.
6 I'm .... in studying science. I'd like to be a scientist.
7 I'm .... at swimming but I don't like sports like badminton.
8 I'm .... to watching my favourite football team play tonight.

Progress test 2 Units 3–4

1 Complete these sentences with the words in the box.

silver   trainers   gloves   plain   jacket   suit

1 My hands are cold. Where are my .... ?

2 My mother bought me a leather .... at the weekend. It looks good with my jeans.

3 Do you like my .... bracelet?

4 My mother usually wears a .... to work - a jacket and skirt, not trousers.

5 I don't like jumpers with stripes or spots. I prefer a .... one.

6 I like running and these are my favourite ....

2 These sentences are comparing things. Complete the sentences with the correct form of the word in brackets.

1 Gold is .... silver. (expensive)

2 My trainers are .... my school shoes. (comfortable)

3 My brother's shoes are .... my shoes. (big)

4 I learn ten different subjects at school. Geography is .... (interesting)

5 My favourite café has .... ice cream in town. (good)

6 That shop has .... milkshakes in the world! (bad)

3 Choose the best word to complete the sentences.

1 My sister won a prize at school who / which was a surprise!

2 I often go to the library which / where I can use the computers.

3 There are a lot of students at my school who / where like sport.

4 My best friend lives in a house which / where is near the river.

5 I like TV programmes which / who are funny.

6 The teacher wanted to find a student who / which was interested in fashion.

4 Complete the sentences with the correct form of the verb in brackets. Use the present perfect or past simple.

1 My sister .... (see) three scary movies so far this week.

2 A new cinema .... (open) in my town last week.

3 My mother .... (make) me a fantastic costume for the fancy dress party last month.

4 I .... (read) all the *Harry Potter* books but I want to read them again.

5 My friends .... (come) to my house three hours ago.

6 My English teacher .... (be) at our school since 2010.

7 My father .... (buy) a new computer yesterday. It's fantastic!

8 My mother .... (go) to visit our grandmother for a few days.

9 .... (you/ever/have) a banana and chocolate milkshake?

10 At the weekend I .... (write) about my visit to London.

5 Complete the sentences with the words in the box.

excited   disappointed   serious   worried jealous   afraid   annoyed   surprised

1 I'm .... of my best friend. She always has fantastic new clothes.

2 We watched the latest Batman film last night but we were very .... in it.

3 My sister has always been .... of spiders.

4 I'm .... about my pet cat. It's really ill.

5 I'm really .... with my brother. He's borrowed my iPod.

6 Are you .... about going to the concert this evening?

7 We were all .... by the ending of the movie. It wasn't what we expected.

8 Is your brother .... about being an actor? I thought he wanted to be a pilot.

6 Choose the best answer (a, b or c) to complete each sentence.

1 We have .... had English and Maths this morning.
a already
b yet
c since

2 We've .... been on the rollercoaster. It was scary!
a never
b just
c since

3 My grandmother has .... seen a scary movie. Can you believe that?
a yet
b since
c never

4 We've lived in this town .... six years.
a since
b ago
c for

5 My mother went to Harrods a month ....
a ago
b since
c yet

6 My football team haven't won a match .... March.
a for
b since
c just

7 Have you been to London ....?
a yet
b ago
c never

8 Up .... last month, I didn't like going on theme park rides.
a since
b until
c for

7 Use a form of the words in capitals to complete each sentence.

1 I didn't do much at the weekend. It was very

....

RELAX

2 At my friend's party, there was an .... He was great!
ENTERTAIN

3 My most .... holiday was in Australia.
ENJOY

4 I wanted Nadal to win the tennis match but he didn't. It was such a ....
DISAPPOINT

5 What was the most .... ride at the theme park?
EXCITE

6 The concert was excellent. The .... were very pleased.
ORGANISE

Progress test 3 Units 5–6

1 Choose the best answer (a, b or c) to complete each sentence.

1 I am very .... I can't run 20 metres!
   a fit
   b fitness
   c unfit

2 Who has the .... diet in your class?
   a health
   b healthiest
   c unhealthy

3 I love .... carrots in my salad. I don't like cooked carrots.
   a fried
   b raw
   c boiled

4 I will go .... learning English after I leave school.
   a back
   b for
   c on

5 My older brother .... eat many vegetables as a child.
   a didn't use to
   b used to
   c used

6 I went to India .... I wanted to see the Taj Mahal.
   a despite
   b because
   c but

7 We arrived at the cinema early .... we went to a café.
   a so
   b because
   c despite

8 We had a fantastic holiday in Scotland .... the rain!
   a although
   b but
   c despite

9 I love fruit, especially ....
   a pineapple
   b spinach
   c lettuce

10 My favourite fish is ....
    a corn
    b cod
    c beef

2 Choose the best form of the future verbs to complete the dialogues.

1 A: My plane *leaves / is going to leave* at 9.00 tomorrow.
   B: OK. *I'm going to take / I'll take* you to the airport.

2 A: I promise *I'm giving / I'll give* you back your biology book on Friday.
   B: Good because *I write / I'm writing* my essay at the weekend.

3 A: What are *you going to do / do you do* when you get up tomorrow morning?
   B: *I play / I'm playing* tennis.

4 A: Next week, *we'll start / we are starting* practising for the marathon.
   B: OK, *I'm buying / I'll buy* some new trainers.

5 A: Ah, you've been to the shops. What are *we having / will we have* for dinner tonight?
   B: Pasta and chicken.

6 A: What do you think you *are studying / will study* when you go to university?
   B: I think *I'll do / I do* English.

Compact Preliminary for Schools by Sue Elliott and Amanda Thomas © Cambridge University Press 2013 **Photocopiable**

3 Match sentence halves a–f with 1–6.

1 I'm mad
2 I'm always dying
3 I can't
4 I'm really
5 There's no
6 I hope we do

a stand cooking. It's so boring!
b way Sam will get into the football team.
c about sport.
d well in the volleyball tournament.
e into history. I love visiting castles.
f for a snack when I get home from school.

4 Complete the sentences with the words in the box.

cosy   freezing   lively
comfortable   friendly   view

Last year we went skiing in France. The weather was snowy and really **(1)** .... We were staying in a large **(2)** .... house. It had six bedrooms and a lovely lounge to relax in. My bedroom wasn't very big but it was warm and **(3)** ....
The **(4)** .... from my bedroom window was fantastic. I could see the Alps! We stayed in an interesting town. There was lots to do in the evening so it was very **(5)** .... Everyone was very **(6)** .... and we met people from lots of different countries.

5 Choose the best word to complete the sentences.

1 A marathon runner *should* / *can't* eat pasta.

2 Students *don't have to* / *mustn't* run in school.

3 We *could* / *must* go swimming tomorrow if it's a nice day. Would you like to?

4 You *shouldn't* / *can* play on the computer for a long time. It's bad for your eyes.

5 Do you want to play tennis in the park? You *mustn't* / *don't have to* pay. It's free.

6 We *must* / *can't* give our homework to the teacher tomorrow or she'll get angry.

7 You *can't* / *should* go to the shop now. It's closed.

8 *Must* / *Can you take* your iPod to school with you? Our teacher told us not to.

6 Complete the sentences with the correct form of the verb in brackets. Use the infinitive or the *-ing* form.

1 I forgot .... (bring) my trainers to school today.

2 I'm looking forward to .... (visit) my friend who lives in a windmill.

3 Can you imagine .... (live) on a boat?

4 I promise .... (tidy) my bedroom after school.

5 My father offered .... (take) my friend and I to the cinema.

6 Do you intend .... (go) to university?

7 Which theme park ride do you suggest .... (try) first?

8 I apologised to my teacher for .... (be) late.

9 I try .... (avoid) cycling in town. It's so busy.

10 My mother taught me how .... (cook) pasta.

7 Complete the sentences with the words in the box. Some words will be used more than once.

go   do   make   have

1 When are you going to .... your homework?

2 I sometimes .... an argument with my sister.

3 When we go on a picnic, my mother and father always .... delicious food.

4 We could .... swimming in the sea if you want.

5 At the restaurant, my parents had fish and I had chicken. I didn't .... the right choice. It wasn't very nice.

6 Do you want to .... camping this summer?

Progress test 4 Units 7–8

1 Choose the best answer (a, b or c) to complete each sentence.

1 This animal has fur and wings.
   a a bat
   b a parrot
   c a penguin

2 If you are a vegetarian, you don't eat
   ....
   a carrots
   b bananas
   c meat

3 It is .... to see animals like white tigers because there are not many of them.
   a wildlife
   b cruel
   c rare

4 If you have done a job for a long time, you are
   ....
   a experienced
   b generous
   c favourite

5 I have a problem and I don't know how to
   .... it.
   a escape
   b solve
   c find

6 My friend .... on some good advice to me about the exam.
   a passed
   b went
   c carried

7 "Are you going to Thailand?" she ....
   a said
   b asked
   c told

8 You don't usually see a lot of water in a
   ....
   a lake
   b beach
   c desert

2 Complete the text with the correct form of the verbs. Use the past simple or past perfect.

An unexpected trip

An 11-year-old boy, Liam, (1) .... (have) an unexpected plane journey last Tuesday. He (2) .... (go) to the shops with his mother in the morning when he (3) .... (become) bored. He (4) .... (be) near Manchester airport and he (5) .... (decide) to go and see the planes. His mother soon (6) .... (tell) the police that he (7) .... (disappear). The British police (8) .... (search) everywhere but by 5.00 they still (9) .... (not find) him. Then the police in Manchester (10) .... (get) a phone call from an airline pilot. Liam (11) .... (board) a plane and was flying to Italy! When airport staff in London (12) .... (see) him, they (13) .... (think) he was with a family so they (14) .... (not ask) him for his passport.

3 Write these sentences in reported speech.

1 "I'm having a great holiday."
   She said ....

2 "I might come and see you."
   He said ....

3 "Will you help me?"
   She asked ....

4 "I haven't been to Canada."
   She said ....

5 "Put your clothes away."
   My mother told ....

6 "I flew to Spain with my mother."
   The boy said ....

4 Complete the sentences with the words in the box. You don't need two of the words.

> crowded   weigh   traffic jam   check in
> speed limit   platform   departure gate
> waves   harbour   flight attendant

1 I stood on the railway station .... and waited for my train.
2 The town was very .... this morning. I think everyone was shopping!
3 I didn't enjoy that boat trip. The .... were really big.
4 How much does your suitcase ....? I hope it's less than 23 kilos.
5 I showed my boarding card to the .... as I got on the plane.
6 Every Friday evening there is a .... It takes my father a long time to drive home.
7 The ship sailed into the .... and we all got off.
8 The .... on the motorway in the UK is 110 kph.

5 Match sentence halves a–f with 1–6.

1 If we don't hurry,
2 If we hurry,
3 If I had the choice,
4 If I have enough money,
5 If I saw my friend on holiday,
6 If I didn't have a computer,

a I'd go to New Zealand on holiday.
b I wouldn't be able to do my homework.
c we'll miss the plane.
d I'd be very happy.
e we won't miss the train.
f I'll go to New Zealand on holiday.

6 Choose the best word(s) to complete the sentences.

1 I was walking to school when I *saw / was seeing* my best friend.
2 The students were working hard when the head teacher was *coming / came* in.
3 I took these photographs while I *was flying / flew* over the Alps.
4 *Were you eating / Did you eat* your dinner when I phoned you last night?
5 I *walked / was walking* in the mountains when it started raining.
6 While I was sunbathing on the beach, a ball *hit / was hitting* me.
7 We *slept / were sleeping* in our tent when we heard a loud bang.
8 I found some interesting flowers while I *walked / was walking* through the forest.

Progress tests key

Progress test 1

1 | 1 e 2 b 3 a 4 f 5 c 6 d

2 | 1 are you doing 2 'm/am watching 3 Do you want
4 are playing 5 'm/am looking 6 visits 7 works
8 is doing 9 make 10 do you usually cook

3 | 1 b 2 a 3 c 4 c 5 a 6 a 7 b 8 c

4 | 1 won 2 in 3 get 4 believes 5 defends
6 succeed 7 lost 8 negative

5 | 1 was feeling 2 was playing 3 was 4 had
5 drove 6 were waiting 7 met 8 were putting
9 gave 10 Did we win?

6 | 1 enjoy 2 afraid 3 can't stand 4 worried
5 fond 6 interested 7 good 8 looking forward

Progress test 2

1 | 1 gloves 2 jacket 3 silver 4 suit 5 plain
6 trainers

2 | 1 more expensive than 2 more comfortable than
3 bigger than 4 the most interesting 5 the best
6 the worst

3 | 1 which 2 where 3 who 4 which 5 which 6 who

4 | 1 has seen 2 opened 3 made 4 have read
5 came 6 has been 7 bought 8 has gone
9 Have you ever had 10 wrote

5 | 1 jealous 2 disappointed 3 afraid 4 worried
5 annoyed 6 excited 7 surprised 8 serious

6 | 1 a 2 b 3 c 4 c 5 a 6 b 7 a 8 b

7 | 1 relaxing 2 entertainer 3 enjoyable
4 disappointment 5 exciting 6 organisers

Progress test 3

1 | 1 c 2 b 3 b 4 c 5 a 6 b 7 a 8 c 9 a 10 b

2 | 1 leaves; I'll take 2 I'll give; I'm writing
3 are you going to do; I'm playing 4 we'll start; I'll buy
5 are we having 6 will study; I'll do

3 | 1 c 2 f 3 a 4 e 5 b 6 d

4 | 1 freezing 2 comfortable 3 cosy 4 view
5 lively 6 friendly

5 | 1 should 2 mustn't 3 could 4 shouldn't
5 don't have to 6 must 7 can't 8 Can

6 | 1 to bring 2 visiting 3 living 4 to tidy 5 to take
6 to go 7 trying 8 being 9 to avoid 10 to cook

7 | 1 do 2 have 3 make 4 go 5 make 6 go

Progress test 4

1 | 1 a 2 c 3 c 4 a 5 b 6 a 7 b 8 c

2 | 1 had 2 had gone 3 became 4 was 5 decided
6 told 7 had disappeared 8 searched 9 hadn't found
10 got 11 had boarded 12 had seen 13 thought
14 didn't ask

3 | 1 She said she was having a great holiday.
2 He said he might come and see me.
3 She asked if I would help her.
4 She said she hadn't been to Canada.
5 My mother told me to put my clothes away.
6 The boy said he had flown to Spain with his mother.

4 | 1 platform 2 crowded 3 waves 4 weigh
5 flight attendant 6 traffic jam 7 harbour 8 speed limit

5 | 1 c 2 e 3 a 4 f 5 d 6 b

6 | 1 saw 2 came 3 was flying 4 Were you eating
5 was walking 6 hit 7 were sleeping 8 was walking

Sample answer sheet: Paper 1

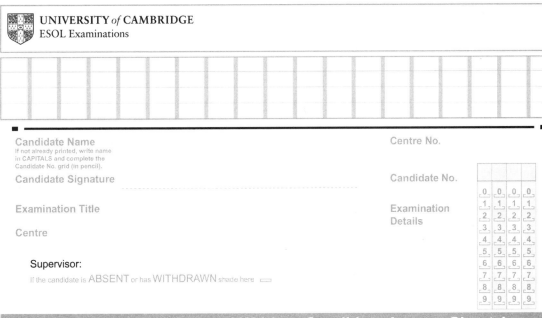

UNIVERSITY *of* **CAMBRIDGE**
ESOL Examinations

Candidate Name
If not already printed, write name in CAPITALS and complete the Candidate No. grid (in pencil).

Candidate Signature

Examination Title

Centre

Supervisor:
If the candidate is ABSENT or has WITHDRAWN shade here ▭

Centre No.

Candidate No.

Examination Details

PET Paper 1 Reading and Writing Candidate Answer Sheet 1

Instructions

Use a PENCIL (B or HB).

Rub out any answer you want to change with an eraser.

For **Reading:**
Mark ONE letter for each question.
For example, if you think **A** is the right answer to the question, mark your answer sheet like this:

Part 1		Part 2		Part 3		Part 4		Part 5	
1 A B C		**6** A B C D E F G H		**11** A B		**21** A B C D		**26** A B C D	
2 A B C		**7** A B C D E F G H		**12** A B		**22** A B C D		**27** A B C D	
3 A B C		**8** A B C D E F G H		**13** A B		**23** A B C D		**28** A B C D	
4 A B C		**9** A B C D E F G H		**14** A B		**24** A B C D		**29** A B C D	
5 A B C		**10** A B C D E F G H		**15** A B		**25** A B C D		**30** A B C D	
				16 A B				**31** A B C D	
				17 A B				**32** A B C D	
				18 A B				**33** A B C D	
				19 A B				**34** A B C D	
				20 A B				**35** A B C D	

Continue on the other side of this sheet ➡

PET RW 1

DP491/389

Sample answer sheet: Paper 1

For **Writing (Parts 1 and 2):**

Write your answers clearly in the spaces provided.

Part 1: Write your answers below.	Do not write here
1	1 1 0
2	1 2 0
3	1 3 0
4	1 4 0
5	1 5 0

Part 2 (Question 6): Write your answer below.

Put your answer to Writing Part 3 on Answer Sheet 2 ➡

Do not write below (Examiner use only).

| 0 | 1 | 2 | 3 | 4 | 5 |

Sample answer sheet: Paper 1

You must write within the grey lines.

Answer only one of the two questions for Part 3.
Tick the box to show which question you have answered.
Write your answer below. Do not write on the barcodes.

Part 3	Question 7		Question 8	

Examiner Mark:

Sample answer sheet: Paper 2

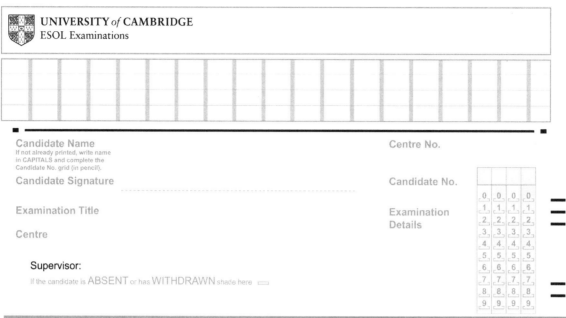

UNIVERSITY of CAMBRIDGE
ESOL Examinations

Candidate Name
If not already printed, write name
in CAPITALS and complete the
Candidate No. grid (in pencil).

Candidate Signature

Examination Title

Centre

Supervisor:
If the candidate is ABSENT or has WITHDRAWN shade here

Centre No.

Candidate No.

Examination
Details

0	0	0	0
1	1	1	1
2	2	2	2
3	3	3	3
4	4	4	4
5	5	5	5
6	6	6	6
7	7	7	7
8	8	8	8
9	9	9	9

PET Paper 2 Listening Candidate Answer Sheet

You must transfer all your answers from the Listening Question Paper to this answer sheet.

Instructions

Use a PENCIL (B or HB).

Rub out any answer you want to change with an eraser.

For **Parts 1, 2** and **4:**
Mark ONE letter for each question.
For example, if you think **A** is the right answer to the
question, mark your answer sheet like this:

For **Part 3:**
Write your answers clearly in the spaces next
to the numbers (14 to 19) like this:

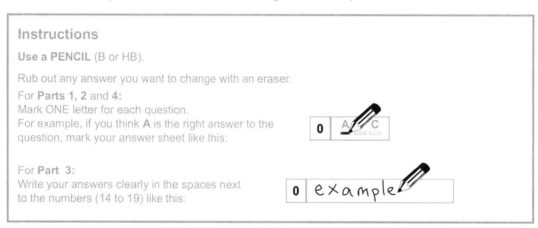

Part 1	Part 2	Part 3	Do not write here	Part 4
1 A B C	8 A B C	14	1 14 0	20 A B
2 A B C	9 A B C	15	1 15 0	21 A B
3 A B C	10 A B C	16	1 16 0	22 A B
4 A B C	11 A B C	17	1 17 0	23 A B
5 A B C	12 A B C	18	1 18 0	24 A B
6 A B C	13 A B C	19	1 19 0	25 A B
7 A B C				

PET L

DP493/391

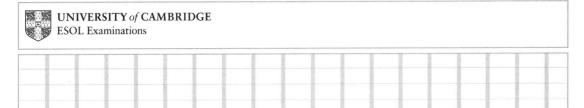

UNIVERSITY *of* **CAMBRIDGE**
ESOL Examinations

Candidate Name
If not already printed, write name
in CAPITALS and complete the
Candidate No. grid (in pencil).

Centre No.

Candidate No.

Examination Title

Examination Details

Centre

Supervisor:
If the candidate is ABSENT or has WITHDRAWN shade here ⊂⊃

0	0	0	0
1	1	1	1
2	2	2	2
3	3	3	3
4	4	4	4
5	5	5	5
6	6	6	6
7	7	7	7
8	8	8	8
9	9	9	9

PET Paper 3 Speaking Mark Sheet

Date of test:

Month   01 02 03 04 05 06 07 08 09 10 11 12

Day   01 02 03 04 05 06 07 08 09 10 11 12 13 14 15 16 17 18 19 20 21 22 23 24 25 26 27 28 29 30 31

Marks awarded:

	0	1.0	1.5	2.0	2.5	3.0	3.5	4.0	4.5	5.0
Grammar and Vocabulary	0	1.0	1.5	2.0	2.5	3.0	3.5	4.0	4.5	5.0
Discourse Management	0	1.0	1.5	2.0	2.5	3.0	3.5	4.0	4.5	5.0
Pronunciation	0	1.0	1.5	2.0	2.5	3.0	3.5	4.0	4.5	5.0
Interactive Communication	0	1.0	1.5	2.0	2.5	3.0	3.5	4.0	4.5	5.0
Global Achievement	0	1.0	1.5	2.0	2.5	3.0	3.5	4.0	4.5	5.0

Test materials used: 1 2 3 4 5 6 7 8 9 10

Assessor's number	**Interlocutor's number**	**Test format**	**Number of 2nd Candidate**	**Number of 3rd Candidate**
A A 0 0 A A	A A 0 0 A A	Examiners : Candidates	0 0 0 0	0 0 0 0
B B 1 1 B B	B B 1 1 B B		1 1 1 1	1 1 1 1
C C 2 2 C C	C C 2 2 C C	2 : 2	2 2 2 2	2 2 2 2
D D 3 3 D D	D D 3 3 D D		3 3 3 3	3 3 3 3
E E 4 4 E E	E E 4 4 E E	2 : 3	4 4 4 4	4 4 4 4
F F 5 5 F F	F F 5 5 F F		5 5 5 5	5 5 5 5
G G 6 6 G G	G G 6 6 G G		6 6 6 6	6 6 6 6
H H 7 7 H H	H H 7 7 H H		7 7 7 7	7 7 7 7
J J 8 8 J J	J J 8 8 J J		8 8 8 8	8 8 8 8
K K 9 9 K K	K K 9 9 K K		9 9 9 9	9 9 9 9

PET S

DP383/332

Photocopiable resources

Unit 2, Listening, Exam task

Recording script

You will hear a man called Don Wood talking about a special sports school on the radio.

For each question, fill in the missing information in the numbered space.

Thanks very much for the opportunity to tell your listeners about the International Sports Academy or ISA in Florida, USA. My name's Don Wood and I'm a senior coach at ISA, one of the best sports schools in the world. We have 500 talented young athletes aged 12 to 18 studying with us from dozens of countries. You can find out if you've got what it takes to join ISA by coming to an interview on April 22 when we're going to select possible new students for next year, which begins on September 15th. If you'd like to be there you can phone my assistant Leo Hawkins that's H A W K I N S on 0998 354678.

The programme at ISA is busy and varied. You can choose one main sport from all the usual sports such as soccer or football, tennis, swimming, and also hockey which you can do from the start of the next school year. As well as doing normal school lessons, you spend ten hours a week practising your main sport after school. Many of our students also spend the weekends at tournaments all over the USA. As well as your training programme we expect you to find time for homework. And if you need extra help with English, we have classes in that too. Students also learn how to perform well in competitions – that means learning to control the mind, as well as making sure they are strong and fit enough to compete.

So life at ISA is really busy. You need to enjoy a challenge and be very organised. But you don't need to worry about how you'll manage being away from home for the first time. Each student has a personal coach who helps them manage their time and talks about any problems they may have.

If you're talented, confident and believe in yourself, give us a call.

Unit 4, Listening, Exam task

Recording script

There are seven questions in this part. For each question, there are three pictures and a short recording. For each question, choose the correct answer A, B or C.

1   *What time does the film start?*

Boy: What time does the film start this evening, Mum?

Mum: Not until quarter to eight. I thought it started at quarter past seven but that was another film. Anyway we need to be at the cinema by half past seven because there's always a queue to collect the tickets and get drinks.

Boy: So, we won't need to leave here until seven fifteen then.

Mum: No. That should give us plenty of time.

2   *What did Jenny buy at the film festival?*

Boy: Did you get that T-shirt at the film festival Jenny?

Jenny: I've had this one for ages actually. There were loads of really cool T-shirts there but all much too expensive. The only thing I could afford was a poster but I haven't put it up on my wall yet.

Boy: Did you get any famous actors to sign it?

Girl: No, unfortunately. I wanted to but they were only signing copies of their books.

3   *Which instrument has the boy recently started learning?*

Woman: So Jack, how are you getting on with your music lessons?

Jack: Well, I'm finding the violin quite hard at the moment. It was easy to begin with but now I've got to a higher level, it's much more challenging.

Woman: And you're also studying the trumpet, right?

Jack: That's what I wanted to learn but there wasn't a teacher available so I took up the flute a few months ago instead. I'm enjoying it and I really like my teacher.

4   *How did the family travel to the concert?*

Woman: Did I tell you we almost missed the concert? I told everyone to be ready really early because I was worried about the traffic. So everyone was in the car and guess what? It wouldn't start. I couldn't believe it. There wasn't a bus until the following day and the train only went as far as Lipton and then you had to go by taxi. There were no hire cars available either so in the end our very kind neighbour lent us his and we just got there in time.

5   *Which circus tickets did the man decide to buy?*

Man: There wasn't much choice of circus tickets. There weren't enough of the £12.50 seats for all of us, which is what I was planning to buy. And although there were lots of seats at £14.95, these were only on weekday afternoons, which I know wasn't an option for us. So I'm afraid I've gone for the ones at £17.00. I know it's more than we wanted to pay, but at least we won't be right at the back.

Compact Preliminary for Schools by Sue Elliott and Amanda Thomas © Cambridge University Press 2013   **Photocopiable**

6	*What do the speakers decide to watch on TV?*
Granddad:	There's an interesting documentary about sharks on in half an hour.
Girl:	I think I've already seen it, Granddad. It's really good. I don't mind watching it again. But don't you want to watch the football?
Granddad:	It's not on until very late. I may be too tired to watch it.
Girl:	The Lenny Adams show is on at 9.00. He's very funny. You like him too, don't you?
Granddad:	Umm, I'd rather watch the documentary if you're sure you don't mind seeing it again.
Girl:	No that's fine, Granddad.

7	*Who do the speakers think will win the singing competition?*
Girl:	Who do you think will win the singing competition?
Boy:	I think the one with short dark hair is best.
Girl:	Do you? I think the tall one with the long curly hair has a much better voice.
Boy:	But he sang a really boring song – and he can't dance.
Girl:	That's true. I expect you're right. The others weren't very good, were they?
Boy:	Especially the one with blond hair. He's really annoying. He doesn't have a chance.
Girl:	I agree. But he tried really hard.

Now of course we're not bringing any cooking equipment like a camping cooker or a frying pan, so you're going to learn how to cook your food on a hot rock, which is heated underneath by fire. It's a bit slower than using a normal cooker but works surprisingly well.

Now what about drinks? You'll have to live without juices and hot chocolate, I'm afraid. You'll get all the water you need from rivers and streams but you must remember to boil it for at least three minutes to make sure it's safe to drink.

Right, so before I continue, I'll answer any questions you've got about food. By the way there's a very good website which ...

Unit 5, Listening, Exam task

Recording script

You will hear a man called Pete Russell giving a talk about an extreme camping trip. For each question, fill in the missing information in the numbered space.

OK everyone. Thanks for coming along to find out about our extreme camping trip. Before I start, can I remind you about the training day? Because it will probably rain tomorrow, we've decided to do this on Saturday instead of Thursday. If you want to come on the trip, you must attend. We're starting at 8.30, so make sure you're there on time.

There are different ways to experience extreme camping, but on our trip it means bringing no food or water with you. We're going to eat only what nature can provide. But don't worry, I'm sure you won't be hungry. We're camping at Sandy River and it's easy to find lots of delicious fruit and vegetables nearby, which you can eat raw. I expect some of these will be quite unfamiliar to you, but your guide will make sure you only eat what's safe.

There are also other types of food you can find. The guide will show you where to look for eggs. There are other places you can look for these apart from trees. For example, some birds leave them in holes in the ground or in the grass like snakes do.

Something that's surprisingly good to eat is insects. These are really good for you and actually very tasty. And I'm not talking about flies and wasps – the ones I'm talking about are much bigger. I promise you'll love them!

Because you really have to be an expert to be successful, one thing you won't have to do on this trip is hunting. You don't want to waste time and end up with nothing to eat.

Acknowledgements

Author acknowledgements

The authors would like to thank their editors Judith Greet, Clare Nielsen-Marsh and Ann-Marie Murphy for their useful input and hard work. Many thanks also to Linda Matthews (production controller), Dawn Preston (proof reader).

Sue Elliott would like to give thanks to her lovely children for their tolerance, and to her co-author Amanda for her help and support.

Publisher acknowledgements

The authors and publishers are grateful to the following for reviewing the material during the writing process:
Susan Wilkinson: France; Cressida Hicks, Jane Hoatson, Jessica Smith, Catherine Toomey: Italy; Laura Clyde, Sarah Hellawell: Spain; Cagri Gungormus Yersel: Turkey; Katherine Bilsborough, Annie Broadhead, Felicity O'Dell, Rebecca Raynes, James Terrett: UK.

Development of this publication has made use of the Cambridge English Corpus (CEC). The CEC is a computer database of contemporary spoken and written English, which currently stands at over one billion words. It includes British English, American English and other varieties of English. It also includes the Cambridge Learner Corpus, developed in collaboration with the University of Cambridge ESOL Examinations. Cambridge University Press has built up the CEC to provide evidence about language use that helps to produce better language teaching materials.

This product is informed by the English Vocabulary Profile, built as part of English Profile, a collaborative programme designed to enhance the learning, teaching and assessment of English worldwide. Its main funding partners are Cambridge University Press and Cambridge ESOL and its aim is to create a 'profile' for English linked to the Common European Framework of Reference for Languages (CEFR). English Profile outcomes, such as the English Vocabulary Profile, will provide detailed information about the language that learners can be expected to demonstrate at each CEFR level, offering a clear benchmark for learners' proficiency. For more information, please visit www.englishprofile.org

Photo acknowledgements

The authors and publishers acknowledge the following sources of copyright material and are grateful for the permissions granted. While every effort has been made, it has not always been possible to identify the sources of all the material used, or to trace all copyright holders. If any omissions are brought to our notice, we will be happy to include the appropriate acknowledgements on reprinting.

p. 17(L): Alamy©Janine Wiedel Photolibrary; p. 17(R): ©Corbis Super RF/Alamy; p.18(L): Alamy/©economic images; p. 18(R): Alamy/©Alex Segre; p.24: Rex Features/Startraks Photo; p. 36(L): Alamy/©Photoshot Holdings Ltd; p. 36(R): Shutterstock.com/Sura Nualpradid; p. 40(L): Superstock/©Eye Ubiquitous; p. 40(R): Rex Features/LEHTIKUVA OY

Illustrations by:

pp. 15, 33: Kate Rochester (Pickled Ink)

Design, layout and art edited by:

Wild Apple Design Ltd.